W9-AHG-681

HEROES

100
STORIES
OF
LIVING
WITH
KIDNEY
FAILURE

Copyright © 1998, Grosvenor House Press Inc.

All rights reserved. No part of this publication may be repro-
duced or transmitted in any form or by any means, electronic
or mechanical, including photocopy, recording or any information storage or retrieval system now known or to be
invented, without permission in writing from the publisher,
except by a reviewer who wishes to quote brief passages in
connection with a review written for inclusion in a maga-
zine, newspaper or broadcast.

Canadian Cataloguing in Publication Data

Main entry under title:
Heroes

100 Stories of Living With Kidney Failure
ISBN 1-895-995-18-3

Published by:
            Grosvenor House Press Inc.

1456 Sherbrooke Street West   King West Centre
3rd Floor   2 Pardee, Suite 203
Montréal, Québec   Toronto, Ontario
H3G 1K4   M6K 3H5

The publisher and the creators have used their best efforts
to provide accurate information at the time of printing. The
creators and Grosvenor House Press hereby disclaim all
responsibility for any loss suffered by any person in the light
of future discoveries in this field, and of any omissions or
errors in the text.

Grosvenor House Inc.

TO
THE
HEALING
POWER
OF
STORIES

In order to publish *Heroes*, the *Heroes* Project Team raised funds in the hospital, renal and business communities and without their support this book would not have been created.

B.G.L. Brokerage Ltd.
Bristol Myers Squibb Pharmaceutical
    Group
Nellie Cecilia Brayne
Fresenius Medical Care
Fujisawa Canada Inc.
Grosvenor House Press Inc.
Hoffman-LaRoche Inc.
Hospal–Gambro
In loving memory of Eddie Hymovitch
Janssen-Ortho Inc.
Kidney Fund, Royal Victoria Hospital
Kidney Foundation of Canada,
    Québec Branch
Merck Frosst Canada Inc.
Novartis Pharmaceuticals Canada Inc.
Pegasus Healthcare International
Hyman Rabinovitch
Royal Victoria Hospital:
    Audio Visual Department
    Patients' Committee
    Patient Education Committee
Somiper
The Kendall Company, Manufacturer
    and Distributor of the Quinton® and
    Accurate dialysis catheters
Trenmore Printing

Thank You!

Foreword

This book contains 100 stories told by people (and sometimes family members) with end-stage renal disease. While the stories all come from one dialysis unit, they represent a cross section of the kind of experiences that might be found in any dialysis unit in Canada or any other country. Some people chose to write out their own stories, others preferred to be interviewed and then to change the transcript as they wished. Everyone openly shared their struggles, pain, joy, and coping strategies so that others could benefit. While the book has been edited to reduce it to a manageable size, great care was taken to ensure that each story remains true to the first-hand account provided by each author.

There are many benefits that we hope will flow from this project. First, there is acknowledgment of those who have told their stories. People with end-stage renal disease face difficulties and odds as overwhelming as soldiers in battle, arctic explorers, or cosmonauts in space. Recognition of this heroism gives their struggle meaning that might otherwise be lost. The second benefit is to those who read the book. We are certain that people, in particular other patients, will be supported and inspired by reading about those who have had similar experiences and will learn things often omitted from "expert" descriptions (such as those found in medical textbooks or told by kidney disease specialists). The project also has a third dimension—it is primarily through storytelling that individuals can begin to create a common culture and share a sense of community. This book may contribute to an improved quality of life for those with kidney failure by opening the way for greater mutual support, advocacy for improved treatment, and public recognition of patients' needs.

Some of the stories are happy, some of them are sad, most of the stories have their share of challenges and difficulties. They are all characterized by heroism, hope and courage. Enjoy them as a gift from the Heroes and the Heroes Project Team.

Brian E. Ditty, a 34-year-old man, began treatment 15 years ago.
His treatments have been hemodialysis and two kidney transplants.

I was 15 years old when I was told my kidneys were shrinking and I certainly did not know what dialysis was, so they suggested I visit a dialysis unit in the future. I got a fistula put in my left arm when I was 16 years old at the Montreal Children's Hospital. These are created under a local anaesthetic and are used to connect you to the dialysis machine. I thought they were pretty neat because they made a buzzing sound and I could fool my friends with it. I would tell them it was a motor to keep my blood going, that I was stronger and faster. This gave me great pleasure.

When I was in grade 11 they told me I should go visit a dialysis unit now because my creatinine was getting too high. My mother made an appointment for me to go see the dialysis unit. My mother took me out to lunch for some pizza nearby, and then we visited the unit. We walked into the unit and all I saw was old people, and they looked terrible. I was thinking to myself, "This is what I am going in for?" I left very quickly and as soon as I got outside I threw up all over the sidewalk. I guess I was a little more upset than I thought. So I blocked the whole thing out of my mind, graduated from high school and started college. When I was 18 years  old they transferred me to the hospital where I kept going in for blood tests once a week; they were monitoring me very closely now. I was 19 when my doctor called me and said it was time to start dialysis. I told him, "No, I don't think so, it's not for me."

He said, "What do you mean, what are you talking about?" I told him again, "It's not for me, it's not my lifestyle." He then told me if I did not start I would die in a few weeks. I told him that was fine, I'd had a good life.

When I got off the phone my mother asked me who it was. I told her it was the doctor and he wanted me to start dialysis and I said it was not going to happen. My parents then got together and put the pressure on me. I saw that they were very upset, so I decided to start and called the doctor back and told him. He was very relieved.

I made an appointment for my first treatment at the dialysis unit. My mother and I arrived and looked in. The people were middle-aged but to me they still looked old. They got me a lazyboy chair and sat me down beside two of the nicest guys, Ray and Armando. These two guys helped set me up with how I would deal with dialysis and everything that goes along with it. They started off with humor right away. They told me I could drink all the beer I wanted now.

I sat down and was connected to the machine. They used these gigantic needles at the time—they were like nails. That's the reason you get a fistula, to enlarge your veins to accept the needles. One is to take the blood out and the other is to return it. One minute after being on the machine I passed out and when I woke up I said to myself, "Is this going to happen all the time?" Ray and Armando just made a joke of it, and I thought well, this is not so bad, these guys are pretty cool for old guys.

I was on dialysis for just over two years when I got my first transplant. During that time they removed both my kidneys because they thought they might cause an infection. In retrospect this operation was the most painful and hardest to recover from, even more so than the two transplants and all the tests and procedures. I did not think about it back then but now I wish I would have kept my old kidneys, just in case something were to come around in modern medicine and they could revive them. Also during this time period my parents and older brother got tested as possible donors. My little brother wanted to but he was too young.

Nobody was a suitable donor for reasons that are not important. The important thing I learned about myself during this time was that I did not believe in live donors. From that point on I decided I would only take cadaver kidneys. It's something everybody should get straight in their heads early. I feel it is a huge responsibility and emotional debt that could never be paid back.

I was always on hemodialysis. I did not like the idea of CAPD. I did not like having my sickness around me 24 hours a day. With CAPD you have to give yourself the treatment at least four times a day and the supplies would be stored in your house. You would also have to create a sterile environment for every treatment. This was not for me. I like the freedom of coming into the hospital every second day, having my treatment then blowing it off until the next session. That way I could go about my business. Mind you the treatments were six hours at a time for me back then.

I tried to stay in college but it was really hard. Dialysis took a lot out of me. I remember once in the winter I was coming home on the bus after a dialysis treatment, and I was really wiped out. I was standing in the aisle holding onto the handrail. I passed out in the aisle and when I was coming to, I heard these old ladies and men saying to each other "Look at that drunken teenager, isn't it disgusting? Look at how kids are today with no parents and no future." I wanted to say something but I was always taught to respect my elders. One thing I did say to myself was how people make quick judgements about situations they know nothing about.

During my first stint on dialysis I met a woman. I started dating her and she was with me the whole time on dialysis and through my first transplant, which I got when I was 21. When I was transplanted my parents were very stressed out and I did not think they could take much more, so this woman I'd met (now my girlfriend) asked me if I would move in with her. She did everything for me and more. Because she worked in the hospital she would tell me about how I was doing, when I was going to be called, and not to worry about this or that. She took care of me when I wasn't feeling well and explained everything that was going to happen. I am the type of person that needs to know the reasons why things happen or I don't feel comfortable. Eventually we broke up because I felt I owed her so much and would never have been able to pay her back in my lifetime.

After the transplant, I finished college and went to university. Then I started working at my father's company until I decided to start my own design and construction company.

About 10 years into my transplant, I developed high blood pressure and started taking medication. This is common with transplant patients. However, my blood pressure kept getting higher. During this time I fell through a roof at work and damaged my fistula beyond repair. Three weeks later the doctor told me they would have to start some invasive procedures to reduce my blood pressure. The doctor gave me three options. One was to do nothing and the high blood pressure would eventually kill the kidney. The second option was an angioplasty which had some risks, and the final option was a bypass operation. I went home and talked it over with my parents. They basically just listened because they knew I would have to make the decision for myself and live with the consequences. I decided to go with the angioplasty; it sounded good, it sounded easy, and it sounded quick.

I had a bad feeling when I was lying on the operating table. The whole thing took about an hour, then I was brought up to my room where my artery they were using blew open and the whole left side of my body started swelling up with blood. So they called in a vascular surgeon, his team took me down to surgery to repair the artery and I was then taken back to my room where the artery blew open again. They brought me down again, anesthetized me once again, did some more repairs and sent me back up to my room. Because of all the trauma to my vascular system, they decided I needed to have the bypass operation right away or I would lose my kidney.

So for the third time in one day I was anesthetized. By this time my signature on the consent form looked like some ancient language. During that operation I lost the kidney because the blood supply to the kidney was shut off too long. Having the angioplasty was a calculated risk. That's why you have to make your own decisions because only you live with the consequences.

I was in the ICU for about two weeks unconscious and on dialysis. My family really thought I was not going to make it this time, and my father was saying that to some of my ex-girlfriends. So a few of them came to see me, some of whom I had not seen in five or six years. I didn't even know why they were there. It was all quite funny to me.

Losing my kidney and going back onto dialysis was the hardest thing in my life but I had to deal with it. When I started the first time, I was just a teenager and didn't know any better. But this time it was different. When I came in the ICU and they told me I had to start dialysis again I cried for half a day. So I called home and talked with my older brother who calmed me down and assured me things were going to work out. I knew in my mind that transplants don't last forever, even though doctors would like you to think so when you get it.

I was doing dialysis, but since I lost my fistula they had to dialyze me through an artery in my neck with a catheter they call a Sorensen. They tried to create another fistula in my right arm but it failed. Then they told me I would have to be dialyzed through a permcath, which is basically a Sorensen but the tubes coming out of the chest are more permanent and less conspicuous. After doing dialysis this way I realized I probably would not have tolerated going back to using needles. It really wasn't that bad. I would go in for my dialysis every second day for four hours at a time and they would just unscrew the caps at the end of the tubes and connect me to the machine.

It was going along fine until I got my first infection for which I took antibiotics, then I got a second infection and a third. To make a long story a little shorter, I ended up with five permcaths and my body was now resistant to almost all antibiotics. They just kept taking the old permcaths out and putting new ones in. You see it is a catch 22; if there's an infection in your system it infects the new catheter, but you can't take it out because you need a permanent place to dialyze from.

One of the reactions to an infection happened just after I was put on a machine; the nurse was still standing around the machine making some final adjustments when I started to feel really bad. I started to throw up and found it hard to breathe. Shortly after that I stopped breathing and a code 99 was called on me. I was told that I stopped breathing for a little over a minute and everyone in the unit was running around trying to keep the other patients from passing out because of all of the excitement. I guess I started a trend. All I could remember was my doctor talking in my ear telling me to come back, that she wasn't going to lose a patient.

I ended up in the ICU and returned to the unit the next day to assure everyone I was all right. They said, "What are you doing down here, you're supposed to be in ICU. You were dead yesterday."

I was released shortly after but started getting an infection again. They were treating me but my body was too immune to the antibiotics by now. I was at home when I started to react to another infection. It was voting day for the referendum on separation. I was sitting at home when I started developing a fever. It got to 42° Celsius and I was shaking, sweating and throwing up. My brother and mother said I had to go to the hospital. I told them, "No, no, not until I vote." I ended up casting my ballot and going straight to the hospital.

I went to the dialysis unit because it was faster than the ER. I remember a nurse getting the examining room ready for me when I just passed out right in front of her while sitting in a wheelchair. I recovered quickly and got up on the gurney, where I stopped breathing periodically, and when I was breathing I was shaking and sweating. The doctor at that time decided to call another code on me because it was too dangerous to try to transfer me to the ICU without the code team and their equipment, which turned out to be a good decision, because I stopped breathing again en route to the ICU. They injected some kind of medication into my heart that was so painful you could not help but breathe.

I got the feeling that the doctors could not pinpoint the reason why I would stop breathing, but they made up a reason telling me that the infections around my catheter would release themselves or be released when I was connected to the machine and attack my respiratory system. By this time they had decided to remove my permcath completely for a couple of weeks until there was no sign of infection. During this time I was being dialyzed through the groin. They would insert a catheter for each treatment and remove it after. This went on every second day for a week and a half.

At this point they were talking about CAPD. I refused the CAPD, and they agreed to try to get one more catheter into me. When I was in the operating room the surgeon told me that I would either come out with a catheter for hemodialysis or CAPD dialysis. Both were maybes at this point in time. The catheter for the CAPD goes in through your stomach and they probably could not have gotten to the peritoneum because I had a lot of scar tissue.

I said to them if they could not get a hemodialysis catheter in me don't bother waking me. They replied they could not do that and I said, "I'll just quit dialysis." A couple of my doctors were called and they talked to me, and I decided to let them do what they could. The first thing I did in the recovery room was to start feeling around to find out where the tubes were coming out from. I found the permcath for hemo and was very happy.

By this time my doctors were in contact with the Québec transplant society trying to get me on the emergency transplant list because I had lost all access sites, had recurring infections, and had become immune to all the antibiotics. My options had run out.

I was notified by my doctors that they had accepted me on the list and the call came three months later for my kidney. It ended my over-two-and-a-half year wait. You never know when a kidney will come for you and it may never come, so you have to make your peace with dialysis whether you're transplanted or not. You can't put your life on hold until a kidney comes in, even though it's easy to fall into that situation, which I did during my second stint on dialysis until a fellow patient told me about all the things she was doing with her life. This was the catalyst that sent me back to school to learn computers.

About eight hours after my transplant I got out of bed. I wanted to get going. I was proud I was up already. I had places to go and people to see plus I wanted to be out of bed before the nurses told me. The kidney did not start working right away, they called it a "lazy kidney". That's what the doctors call it because they really do not know why some start right away and some start up days, maybe even weeks later.

Mine started up a couple of days later and I was released from hospital six days later. I wanted to beat the record for the shortest stay but ended up tying it. From that point on everything's been just fine. You just have to take care of yourself and take your pills. I would be remiss if I did not mention the physical changes in my looks from the side effects of the drugs I take to keep the kidney alive. It might not sound important compared to the gift you get, but it is a factor I have to deal with.

I believe now you just do what you have to do to stay alive. You get your priorities straight and all the little things in life don't matter anymore. Someone once asked me why little things don't bother me. I told them to have a transplant.

I always look at the good side of things now because if dialysis had not been invented and transplants had not been done I would have been dead at 19, so the rest is just one big bonus.

2

Sabrina Kriegs, a 39-year-old woman, began treatment a year and a half ago. Her treatments have included peritoneal dialysis, hemodialysis and a kidney transplant.

I have recently had a kidney transplant after 16 months of peritoneal dialysis and eight weeks of hemodialysis. From where I am standing now, I am a very lucky person. I was talking to a man in hemo not too long ago, who is a long-term diabetic like myself. His vision is very poor, he can only see shapes, but no detail, he had a walking stick to help him walk. He had been told he isn't able to have a kidney transplant and that he will be on hemo for the rest of his life. As I listened to his story I really felt for him. His story, except for the sequence of events, could have been and nearly was my story.

Four years ago I too was losing my vision, with one eye I could only see shapes and with the other I could not see much better. I would gather all the photos I had of my son who was five years old at the time, and with a magnifying glass I would go over every detail of his face, so scared that I would never see him as he grew up. I would say to myself, "This can't be happening to me!" It had all come on so suddenly. I had been diabetic for many years but my health was good, when my health started to change I didn't realize it was the beginning of kidney failure. The first sign was my eyes. I started tripping on curbs, and misjudging distance, I started seeing black floating lines in my field of vision. From then things went from bad to worse very quickly. Within a month I couldn't pick out my son in a group just two yards away. I was diagnosed with failing kidneys and retinopathy. Laser treatment was started on my eyes. I didn't take the kidney thing too seriously at this point as the problems with my eyes over-shadowed everything. I thought, "At least the kidney problem has been discovered in time and it can just be treated and fixed." Dialysis didn't even enter my mind at this point. I tried to put on a brave face for everyone, but my spirit was sinking. I felt very alone even though I was surrounded by family and friends. How could they relate to what was happening to me, what I was going through, and what I was losing? I covered up a lot of the fear I was feeling. I didn't want people feeling sorry for me on top of everything else. I couldn't have handled that. It would have taken away my "front".

The next stage was accepting that dialysis would be pending sooner than later. I remember my doctor saying to me, "You are a very ill person." I responded by saying, "You're talking like I'm going to be on dialysis in six weeks, or six months." She didn't say no. I asked her, "What's going to happen to me? Am I going to be blind and on a machine for the rest of my life?" Again she didn't say no. I had been told by another doctor that I wasn't a candidate for a transplant because I was diabetic and that hemodialysis would be my only choice.

I was very scared, I wasn't ready yet to choose the day that would be "the first day of the rest of my life". You tend to confuse "choice" with "control". As long as I could choose to put off dialysis, I felt I still had control over my situation. So I continued to go to work and try to cope with my changing abilities, letting myself get sicker and sicker. It's amazing what we will put ourselves through out of fear. It was then that I had decided, if I don't have a choice about my treatment, at least I have a choice about the hospital and the doctors that will treat me. It was the best decision I had made in a long time. I was very sick when I arrived at the emergency room of the hospital. But things turned around very quickly. I was told I did have choices, about my treatment, about a transplant, and about my life. This positive information didn't make my kidney problems disappear, but my spirits rose, which is what I needed to get me to the next hurdle and let myself start the treatment I desperately needed.

I started dialysis in May 1995, and started feeling better right away, as all the toxins that had built up could finally be filtered out. My life was starting to get back to normal. I was back at work. Work was very important for me. It was one of those things that made my life seem "normal"—even if I didn't always have the energy for it. Before coming back to Canada in 1994 due to my health, I had been living in California for 16 years. I had two jobs, worked 55 hours a week (before I had my son) and still had the energy to go out with friends. Now I'd finish work and collapse on the bus on my way home.

Things were getting worse for me. I started having a lot of trouble with my legs and walking was becoming difficult. I found it hard at times to coordinate my muscles. I had developed a very strange walking pattern. On top of this, after being on peritoneal for 16 months I got an infection and on top of that my catheter was blocked. All of which put me in the hospital for a week. I was going to have to start hemodialysis. I felt my spirits sinking again. I was moving farther and farther from my so-called "normal" life, and recognizing myself less and less, both physically and mentally. It's strange, but I found that sometimes when I was in the hospital I felt safe. I could let down my guard, I didn't have to try to look well, which was a struggle. It's okay not to look well in the hospital, but when you're "out there" feeling the way you do, struggling to hang on to your everyday life and who you used to be, that's when you realize how different you feel.

I was on hemo for eight weeks. It was very overwhelming the first few times. The nurses were working so quickly, attaching tubes to tubes, pumping in this and that. So here I was, my vision was saved by laser treatment, I had the choice of peritoneal and I was on the transplant list, and now, trying to keep my spirits up about my legs. A wonderful doctor tried very hard to get me on an emergency transplant list, but as I was not a life-or-death situation it was not possible. I felt lost in the sea of names and blood types that waited like me for a kidney. I couldn't face hemo long-term, so I pleaded my case to go back to peritoneal. The surgery was planned for the next Friday. Wednesday morning at 4:00 a.m., the ringing of the phone woke me up. A woman's voice said, "We have a kidney for you", just like that. I couldn't believe what I was hearing.

Even now as I say the words my heart jumps and flutters. They were the best words I'd heard in a long time.

I went into the operating room smiling. A nurse said to me, "This is a major operation, you could at least be a little nervous!" I told her, "I am so ready for this!" I had found out that I had been on the transplant list for 10 months, but for me I had been waiting for four years for that kidney. The morning after the transplant I felt like a different person. There wasn't much discomfort at all. Even the scar didn't look bad. It's my happy scar. I was sitting in a chair that same day, walking the ward the next day and ready to go home. I was like, "Let me out, I've got a life to live!" I was out in a week.

Although I have stopped announcing when I have to "go", I find myself telling total strangers on the bus, at the grocery store, in elevators, "I just had a kidney transplant a few weeks ago and I feel great, because someone was caring enough to be a donor and give me this chance!" Because you are not given information about the donor, I feel that each time I tell someone I'm saying out loud, "thank you" to my donor.

My son would say to me, "If I could change anything I'd make it so you weren't diabetic and then you wouldn't have lost your kidneys." It's wonderful how kids can say just the right thing at the right time. Max said to me one day while I was setting up my dialysis, "Mum, you're lucky they invented dialysis or you might not be here with me." I had been feeling a little sorry for myself and maybe he sensed that. What he said rang true. Dialysis wasn't taking away my life, kidney failure was doing that. Dialysis was giving me a life.

The support and love from my family helped Max and me through this time, and now things are going to get better and better. The minute I came home from the hospital, Max said straight away, "Do you have more energy now Mum? Can we go for a really long walk, or a bike ride?" I found a picture he had drawn while I was in the hospital. We were riding our bikes, my hair was flying straight back because we were going so fast.

Do I have the same outlook on life as I did before I was sick? I think so. I have always tried to be a positive person. If something gets me down, I try not to stay there too long. I talk it through in my mind until I come to a better outlook on whatever it is. But I do appreciate a lot of the little things in life more, like being able to carry a bag of groceries, walking a mile in 20 minutes rather than an hour, feeling tired because you've had the energy in the day to do something exhausting, not because you are exhausted, drinking as much water as you want, eating bananas, not sucking on ice cubes, walking with Max, even cleaning. So many things we take for granted everyday... they hold my biggest rewards. I have always believed in fate and destiny and although it has been tested during these four years, I believe there is a plan for us all. You just don't always get it proven to you as I have, you must stay on your path and trust your inner voice. I came so close to losing so much. Now, I have my vision, I have my kidney and I can hardly remember that strange walk I developed. I am a very fortunate person. I always say, "I'm like a cat with nine lives."

3

Dimitra Boufonos, a 29-year-old woman, began treatment three years ago. Her treatment has included hemodialysis and a kidney transplant.

Twenty months after I began dialysis, I got a call for a kidney transplant. I have had this transplant for the past 16 months, and I feel very well. Actually, I feel great! And my life goes on. I'm still in school and studying for my Bachelor of Law. I always knew that I wanted to study and be a corporate lawyer, and to be honest, I did not really feel sick when I was on dialysis because I did not have all the usual symptoms that people have.

However, dialysis did affect my life in one respect. It touched my personal life, in terms of having a personal relationship with a man. While I was on dialysis, I did not date or have a boyfriend. Even if someone pursued me, I did not get involved because I did not want anyone to be stuck with me while I was on dialysis. Apart from that, although it was possible for me to travel, I chose not to do so because I thought that going somewhere to be hooked up to the machine was not much of a vacation. But now that I have had a transplant, I can do all those things once again.

However, getting a transplant did involve some difficulties. The first month after I had my kidney transplant, I went through a terrible time. That was because my kidney was not exactly functioning well, and it was hard to cope with that mentally. I knew that if my transplant did not work out, the only other option was going back to dialysis. I was not in very high spirits for the first few months after my transplant because the medications I was taking had side effects (change in hormones, weight gain and facial hair). After that everything went well and luckily everything is still going well now. Despite the changes, I feel fortunate to have had a kidney transplant and to have been given a second chance at a normal life.

I have a very optimistic outlook on life, and I was never pessimistic about my illness. I knew that one day, I would eventually get a transplant, and my life would go back to normal. I also got a lot of support from my family, who was always there for me, and my friends, who never thought of me as being sick. As for people who are just beginning dialysis now, my advice to them is that they have to stay optimistic. It is difficult to deal with something like this, especially when you are young and it happens very abruptly. In my case, I never even knew that I had kidney failure, but within nine months of being diagnosed, I was on dialysis. It happened so fast that I could not even believe it. I was very frightened when I thought that if I did not begin dialysis, I would die. But I think that it is important for people to keep a very optimistic outlook, and to pray that one day they will receive a kidney. After that, I find that life does go back to normal. However, although that is what happened to me, and my life is now back to normal, I do not think that I will ever feel like a "regular" human being again. I have someone else's organ inside my body, and for that reason I do not think that my life will ever be exactly the same.

P.S. I would like to thank all the doctors and nurses in hemodialysis for their kindness and support throughout my stay at the hospital.

4

Maria Ciampanelli, a 49-year-old woman, began hemodialysis 10 and a half months ago.

I have polycystic kidneys, a disease my mom had. When I was 23 years old, a few cysts were found on my kidney but I was given the impression that it was nothing to be too concerned about. I was always in good health. I always worked. It all started when I began to feel dizzy and tired. I was not really surprised when I found out that I was sick because my mom had the same disease. She never went on dialysis. She fell into a coma and died at the age of 50.

Before I went on dialysis, I had an operation for a fistula but it didn't work because my veins were very small. After about three weeks, I had an artificial vein put into my arm. Many times, when some of the  nurses weren't too careful, my arm would get all swollen and purple when the needle would poke along the sides of the vein. My husband underwent eight months of testing to see if he would be a compatible kidney donor. He was found to be a suitable donor. The hospital called me and arranged a kidney transplant on February 21, 1996. Two weeks before this date, I had another echography done to check if everything was fine before the transplant. The doctors, however, found a lot of stones in my gallbladder. To avoid complications, the stones had to be removed and the transplant was delayed. The nephrologists decided not to perform the transplant but rather to remove my two kidneys. My kidneys were so enlarged that it was as if I was pregnant.

On June 2nd, in a seven-to-nine hour operation, my kidneys and the stones in my gallbladder were removed. After the operation, I had a tube put into me. The color of the liquid in the tube alerted the doctor that something was not right. To check out what was wrong, the doctors removed all the stitches and had me reopened. When the doctor fixed the stitches, he discovered a large mass of cysts underneath the liver which had not been seen before. The mass was removed because it could have become cancerous in several years. A month after this operation, I noticed that bile was coming out of the incision from the operation. I went through many tests until the doctors discovered a hole in my intestine. I had to have a third operation. I was in the hospital for three months and one week. I suffered a lot but I always kept up a good morale. At that time, I always wanted to come home and be with my family. My husband helped me and gave me a lot of support.

My life has changed. I had to quit working. After a fistula had been put in, I delayed going on dialysis for seven or eight months because I was very careful and ate a proper diet. But after a time, I started to feel not well. I started to get a restless feeling in my legs and my ankles began to swell. My blood got dirty and finally I had to go on dialysis. After several sessions on dialysis, I started to feel great.

What helps me cope is support from my family, my good morale, and my hope to get a transplant. I have been through a lot, and I want to get a kidney so that I could feel better. I always think about my mom and how she died when she was 50. Things were not as advanced back then. I'm glad that at least I get to live with this dialysis machine which is like a robot but it is what keeps me alive. My life has changed in the sense that I was very independent before, but now sometimes I need a lot of help.

The hospital has become my second home. The people here are very supportive. They are so human. They are so very nice and I would like to thank everybody.

5

Siméon Likhoray (1917-1997) received hemodialysis for eight months.

Well, I couldn't breathe, so my brother called 911 and they came over. So they took me to the hospital and I was in emergency and they ran tests and everything and they took blood tests and what not. Then they took me upstairs and put me on the monitor in the intensive care because I had also developed a heart problem. Anyways I was there for a few days and the doctor said that they were going to transfer me because I was in need of dialysis and they weren't equipped for it. Then when I came here, they ran all kinds of tests and everything. After that they discharged me and told me what was wrong. They told me that I was going to need dialysis, but only in the near future. They told me that my kidneys were only working one-third. I was home for about two or three weeks, and then I had another attack of not breathing. The same thing happened again, they shipped me to the hospital and they gave me oxygen and got me breathing again and then they shipped me here.

So when I got here, they decided that it was time to give me dialysis so they put me a thing in the neck and they started giving me dialysis. After that, a doctor (the surgeon) came over and she had to put a fistula in. She said that it takes about six to eight weeks and in the meantime I took it in the neck. After that they started on the arm. Some of the nurses have a hard time because my veins, when they see the nurse, they hide. They have a heck of a time, it is not a very comfortable thing.

I had always tried, before this, to drink a glass of water for every waking hour. Well they said you should drink a lot of water but the doctor says that isn't true. That's a grandmother story. Now I just have to watch that I don't have too much liquid each day and that includes everything like if you are going to have a drink of water or coffee or jello. On dialysis I have this diet. It's pretty hard. You see I am a widower, my wife died in 1984 so I have to prepare my own meals. And I'm pretty good with the skillet so I like to eat what I cook. Since I'm on dialysis I think

I lost about 40 pounds. I quit smoking in February. The first time I had trouble breathing was in February.

I don't consider myself a hero, I consider myself sick and that's it. I am accepting it, I have no other alternative eh? And there is no such thing as saying that I'll go somewhere for a couple of weeks. Like on a vacation or something. You have to go through the routine. It has never even entered my mind to go anywhere. I would say that this is the biggest restriction on me.

Well, dialysis is just there. What can I do about it? I have to have it, but I feel much better with it. The only thing is just to listen to your doctor and just don't think of dialysis as a sickness. It is there, you are plagued with it, you are not going to get rid of it. After the first dialysis, then the people know that nothing bad happens from being on the machine. It is there, you can watch the numbers jump around, but other than that... it just doesn't bother you.

6

Laureen Bureau-Gould, a 38-year-old woman, began treatment 11 years ago. Her treatment has been a kidney transplant. Jacqueline Bureau, Laureen's sister, donated her kidney to Laureen.

Laureen: At four years old I was developing a lot of throat infections. My mother was taking me to doctors left, right and center and then at one point she decided that there must be something else wrong with me because I was developing more symptoms than just sore throats. She took me to a pediatrician and at that point I had already developed chronic nephritis. I started treatment in New Brunswick where we lived. This was 34 years ago and the medical system wasn't as advanced so I was flown in a number of times to the hospital where I was blessed with meeting and being treated by the doctor. I was followed by the people in New Brunswick and periodically I would come to Montréal. There were problems because at that time, 34 years ago, they didn't know too much about kidneys so I was a guinea pig for a lot of medicines and a lot of medicines just didn't do anything. They didn't have any cures. I was severely allergic to penicillin as a child and back then penicillin was almost a cure-all but I couldn't touch it. So they went into a lot of other things that just didn't work. I was heavily treated with steroids as a kid. For two years I was on high doses of steroids. I was on cortisone and I did not grow for two years, from six to eight years old which is a major growing period. I lost all my hair. I was retaining water and they used to make the water go into my peritoneal cavity and then I'd have to go to the hospital and be tapped so that they could drain the water out of my stomach. Then my torso was tapped until the water was drained out completely. This procedure had to be done every two to three weeks. When I reached a certain weight I would have to go back to the hospital. It sounds so archaic but anyway this is one of the things that had to be done. I missed half the year in school. I was in and out of the hospital constantly. Mom was pregnant with Jacqui during one of my sickest periods. At that time I had to go to Montréal but my mother couldn't come with me because she was pregnant. They put me on a plane. It was a scary and lonely experience. I have relatives in Montréal and my dad came to see me every two weeks and eventually brought me back home. But that is something in my past, a memory of my disease that really left an impression on me, because I was alone and I was very homesick when I had to be away from home. It's a hard memory for all of us in a way. I was thinking this on the way here. Will we ever get over the emotional part of it? Because it really did affect the whole family.

When I was young I was kind of the odd ball because I was sick and I was missing school a lot. I was very protected of course by my mom because she was so worried. Every time I would touch something I would bruise. We didn't deny that I was sick. I remember Mom used to whip my belly out and say, "Look at this", and show the stretch marks. It was her way of dealing with it.

Jacqui: We had to be open. We all felt in a way that you were a special member of the family. I remember telling my friends that my sister is sick and she's really special. It's almost strange to say and it must sound weird but it was like an asset to our family because we were different and that meant that we had to cope with something bigger than the normal family did. In my perspective it was always something that was good for us.

Laureen: The other day I told my mom that when I was a kid I thought that God was punishing me. But when I told my mom that, she said, "Oh Laureen". But she doesn't realize that it did hit me like that. I really did feel that because I was sick I was bad and I was being punished. As a child I knew that this was something that was hard on my parents. We covered up for each other a lot. I had this very happy face on. Children tend to be so wise and so brave.

Jacqui: I always remember you being that way.

Laureen: I didn't complain at all. Every time I came to see the doctor when I was 18 and getting sick again, I would say that I was fine and that there was nothing wrong with me. Eight years later, when I was first interviewed about going through the process of possibly getting a kidney transplant, the doctor who was head of the transplant department scared the life out of me.

He said, "You're very sick or you wouldn't be here". That was hitting me with reality. I was thinking, oh my God I guess I am. I knew I was sick but I didn't give in to it. It was my way of dealing with it. I always had a happy outlook. I always thought that it's okay, I could be worse. I grew up in the hospital so I saw the reality of illness and how you can see a friend in the bed beside you one day and they're not there the next day.

The first time I came to stay at the hospital, the doctor pointed out to my mom that she was spoiling me and that I was getting to be just awful. He let my mom know that I had to be treated like my other siblings. This was a good lesson for all of us. After that we got back on track. So as a kid I just fell into being just another sibling. That's how I wanted to see myself. I didn't want anyone to say, "Oh, she's sick". I wanted to be normal. Do you know what I'm saying? My family gave me so much love. That's how I was normal. I had such a loving home.

We were all loved and we were all equal. There were six of us. Imagine, six girls. I had friends in high school. I kind of went with the flow but I stayed in the background. I think it was because of the inner conflict of having a disease, not wanting to show anybody in high school that I was sick. I only let my personal friends know. I was a normal kid in that I was taking certain courses and trying to figure out the direction in my life that I wanted to follow. I could say that a part of it was the disease but everyone has those growing pains from 12 to 21 or whatever.

Now I'm a part-time secretary for a church. I'm going to school, true. I'm taking a three-year pastoral intervention college program and it's so interesting. I'm also a mom of two.

And I'm an Avon lady. I keep busy. I would love to work in a hospital with children. When I think of myself being in a professional situation, I always become hindered with the fact that I always have to come to the hospital more than other people. My illness still affects my life. For one thing, I can't get life insurance. Also, I worked at a university for five years part time and they wouldn't put me on permanently because of my illness. I still have a problem with this issue.

The thing with kidney disease is that it's not so evident. It's a very personal and private kind of disease where you have to go around blabbing about your urination functions while you're sitting in the hospital. You don't do this in the real world. I felt very shameful growing up with this illness. When I was seeing the doctor as a young adult he would take blood tests but the tests didn't actually show as much kidney damage as my symptoms showed. I had restless legs syndrome. It was a nightmare. This is an inside jitter. It's a physiological defect that happens through uremia in your system. It affects every part of your body. I was severely symptomatic. I wore turtle necks in 90° weather in the middle of the summer. I had poor circulation. I was itchy. I was orange.

I then started to lose my thought pattern. A woman who worked here on a seven-year study in 1983-1984 surveying patients, happened to be a blessing in disguise. Half the patients she educated and half she didn't. I was one who was educated and at that point I learned that these symptoms were happening because I had a kidney disease. I saw a video and I had questionnaires galore and they would ask if I was experiencing restless legs syndrome symptoms. At that point, I didn't have a name for this condition. I had been living with it for years. I strongly believe in patient education. As I've become older, I have become more able to talk to people through lots of trial and error and I have been able to say what's on my mind and ask questions.

Jacqui: I remember when you were being worked up for dialysis and you were so depressed because you couldn't imagine life on a machine.

Laureen: My parents always knew that eventually I would be dialyzed. I always figured that if I had to be on dialysis I would rather die.

Jacqui: At that time nobody in our family really knew about a transplant.

Laureen: That's right. It was never considered because my parents were always told that I would be on dialysis and that's it. I came home one day in 1984 from an appointment with the doctor and said that I don't have to be dialyzed. Three of my sisters and myself set up a meeting with the doctor which I wasn't allowed to be a part of because I wanted to keep saying, "No no no everything is okay." I was depressed and very lethargic. I was being totally eaten by this disease inside and out.

Jacqui: Terry, our sister, took over and brought us to the doctor's office and he arranged for blood tests. I'm the donor because our blood matched perfectly on eight counts, so I was the obvious choice. I was 20 years old. I wasn't married. I didn't have kids. I was able to do it. Laureen called me at work and asked me, "Would you still like to be the donor if our bloods matched perfectly?" I said, "Yeah, of course, that means they match, right?" I got off the phone and I just started bawling my eyes out. It was really emotional. I had a feeling. I guess we each thought that we would be the one.

Finally it was done on August 8, 1985. We were in the hospital two days before playing backgammon until midnight and watching the Late Night Show. It was fun actually. The night before, though, when I was being prepped for the surgery, I felt like I had no pride left. After I had been shaved, I had an IV put in and I had to have an enema. I felt degraded. It was such an awful feeling and everybody was piling into our room and I just wanted everybody to get out of there. I was afraid that after the surgery I would wake up and my life would be very different. I was afraid that I would be treated like a sick person. I had my own apartment and I lived alone. I was really trying to stress my independence and prove to my parents that I could manage. I was afraid that I was going to lose that. Then we held hands in the morning and when we got up we had to pee first. They had given us their little happiness shot so we were all relaxed. They put us on a stretcher, rolled us down the hall and then they put us in the bay and we were holding hands. People were coming up to us as we were waiting to go into the surgery and saying to us, "You have beautiful eyes", and then that was it. It was over. The one thing I noticed though, which was really disturbing to me, was the difference between the way I was treated and the way Laureen was treated when we were in the hospital. They were treating me like an intelligent person. Because of the fact that I was healthy they were asking me different types of questions than they were asking Laureen. They treated you as if you were stupid.

Laureen: That's what happens when you're in a situation fresh. You can be objective but it's different when you're in it for so long. You basically lose your body to the system.

Jacqui: The time after the transplant was a weird time for me because I was 20 years old and I felt like I had fulfilled my purpose in life. It was a strange feeling. I didn't know where I was going next. You know what it's like when you think of fate and destiny? Ever since I was a kid I was always pondering the question "why am I here?" and then it's like, "that's why you are here". That's exactly why you were born. My mom was pregnant with me when Laureen was the most ill. It's kind of weird looking at all these events. It took a few years to put that question to rest and to try and set new goals and decide that there were other things that I had to do here or else I would have been hit by a car the next day. The reception that I had going back to our church community was so warm. It was almost uncomfortable because I felt like they were putting me up on a pedestal. They said, "Oh, you're so good, you did such a nice thing", and then here are my other sisters, especially my sister Jill who had also gone for the blood work and who would have also done it at the drop of a hat. She was getting pushed aside while I was getting all this attention. It just didn't feel like I deserved that. Up until last year I could not put that into words.

When we had our 10-year anniversary last year I made a speech because I could finally figure out what I went through. I got so emotional two weeks before because I wanted to say what I had to say but I didn't know what it was. It was only then that I realized what it was. I got all this attention and was being praised but it wasn't only me who gave. I was just an equal part of the puzzle. I have been blessed and I know that I have been rewarded and I hope that my other sisters have been rewarded as well. It's like a little angel guiding me, it's true.

Laureen: You are an angel.

Jacqui: More and more people are getting counseling for dealing with illnesses. When you receive a kidney transplant it's not as simple as, okay you're healthy now, and off you go. At first you're scared that your kidney may be rejected and that things may not be going so well, but after several years you're on your own. It doesn't work like that. How do you make the adjustment from one day being seriously ill to the next being considered perfectly normal?

Laureen: It took 10 years for me to realize that, first of all, I'm still sick. A kidney transplant does not cure a disease. I have to come to the hospital once every three months. I have to live like a healthy person but be sick. I can live with that but I have to make the transition. Being very ill was almost like a crutch for me. You have to fold the crutch up and put it in the closet. You have to carry on with your life but because you never had any destiny because you were too damn sick and you just didn't want to see tomorrow, it's hard to build that back up again. It's like I was given another chance and I really had to prove to myself that I was worth it and that I was given this gift of life for a reason. I had so much healing to do on the inside. My physical self is doing terrific. It was the inner stuff, all that garbage from childhood, all the situations that are private in my head and all the medical situations in the hospitals. We're not treated normally. We're sick, therefore we're less of a person. At our transplant anniversary party I was able to stand up in front of all of our loved ones and say thank you. I had to tell everyone that their prayers and their thoughts and just being there meant so much to me. Some of them were there for my mom and dad and some of them were there for us. We were all there for each other. That was a part of my journey. I had to get to that part. Even the doctor, my hero, was there. It was so incredible. It was something that I had to do and thank God I had the opportunity to do it. The dialysis unit is such a close-knit family. I feel like I belong. The medical professionals have been wonderful as well as the dietitian and the social worker. I can't say enough about all those who treated me. In making this book we are bringing forth awareness. We need to educate. Medical technology has advanced so much that I was lucky to have been sick at this time. So lucky indeed that I was able to become a mom. My daughter Amie is nine years old and my son Jacob is three and a half. They're really wonderful children. I was only married a year before the transplant. My husband had absolutely no clue how sick I was because I hid it from him. My parents said to him, "This is a sick woman you're marrying and do you still want to get married and do you know what the consequences are?" He understood that statement because he's logical but he didn't live with me as a kid like my parents did so how could he have realized? Then there was me saying that I was fine. This didn't help matters. But he still married me anyway. He has stuck it out with me through illness and through health and is always there for me.

7

Jessie Quirk, a 73-year-old woman, began hemodialysis seven months ago.

After a visit to my doctor, I was told that my kidneys were not functioning well and I was told dialysis was recommended. I have been diabetic since I was 40 and that might have caused my kidney failure.

When the doctor told me that I had to start dialysis I was not very happy because that treatment meant coming to the hospital three times a week. Lately I cracked my hip bone and I have had to spend the last five months in the hospital. I am what they call a long-term patient and that is not helping my situation at all. I find hemodialysis very long and laying on my bed for three hours in the same position bothers my back a lot. I feel a little bit tired and nauseated when I am done with dialysis. The only thing that I see positive about dialysis is that I am still living.

My sister, who lived with me, made a big difference in helping me cope with dialysis. She was very positive and gave me moral support. She talked to me mostly and comforted me when I felt down. My sister did most of the cooking. We used to take turns until I could not cook because my left hand became paralyzed. Now that I am in the hospital my sister comes to visit me every other day. I told her not to come because I thought it was too much for an 85-year-old woman, but she really wants to come because she cares a lot about me. My two other sisters who live in Toronto come nearly every summer to visit me and I find that comforting. I can't go away now like I used to because I have to have dialysis.

For those who are about to start dialysis they should accept it and adjust themselves to it. I was scared when I was introduced to the dialysis machine but there was nothing really to be scared of. Hemodialysis is long and tiresome but you have to have patience. I should feel fortunate because I am still alive. Hopefully dialysis will let me live to see my grandchildren grow up and get married.

8

A 67-year-old man who wishes to remain anonymous began hemodialysis 20 years ago.

I was 33 years old when I learned that I was approaching end-stage renal failure. Now when I went into end-stage renal failure, when I was 47 years old, the reality was that we were not at all prepared. We knew that there was going to be tubes in my life, but we suddenly encountered numerous physical problems, health problems, which I obviously was not prepared for. I am pretty good at adapting, so with the bit of help I got from the nurses and the reading materials they made available to me, plus my own ability to cope, and of course with the assistance and involvement of my wife and my children, I was able to get through the first months. The first six months are the most difficult, you have all kinds of physical and emotional experiences that are not anticipated, but if the people who are surrounding you are interested in your progress, give you the kind of help that you need, you can get over the hump. Once you are beyond the six-month period I don't think it's really all that difficult, you're pretty well used to all the physical and mental changes that you have to cope with.

I had some other things that were going for me. I had a first-rate position in my profession. I was able to work full-time and run the operation that I was heading without any difficulty. Once I was over the six-month period, and once I was able to understand what was going on around me, and to adapt my schedule to meet my dialysis needs, it really wasn't that difficult. Of course I was fortunate because my family was very helpful, my kids and my wife were there for me, and the people I worked with were outstanding and willing to pitch in to help. I did not want to dwell on my illness, I just moved ahead and did all the things I wanted to do. I could travel, we went to Europe many times while I was on dialysis, I could work full-time, and adapt my schedules to my own needs. It was not easy, but it was doable.

The issue of whether or not I would want a transplant came up, but I rejected it because I was doing so well, what did I need a transplant for? I firmly believed in an old French expression which means effectively that better is sometimes the enemy of good. You know there were a greater number of failures than there are today, and I saw no reason to tempt fate if I was doing well.

It's not fair for me to suggest that I am in the same boat as other people. I was financially secure, I was secure in the work I was doing, I was running a big operation, and I was able to pursue it without any real difficulty. So, in that sense I am not really typical. People get sick, they cope, they don't have the financial means, it's a problem. I never had those problems. Yes, there was a major adjustment to the physical challenges, the health challenges, but once I was able to stabilize after six months, I knew what I was dealing with. Look, I am not suggesting that dialysis was a picnic, we had a lot of physical setbacks, but I adapted to the physical setbacks and I went on. In life you get your challenges and your setbacks, and you have to go ahead, you can't sit back and feel sorry for yourself. I never did and I never will, and we went ahead.

I don't think that anything positive comes out of illness. I used to say that working my way through school was great for me, but it's not true. I think kids that went through university, had a good time, enjoyed themselves, traveled and did whatever, in the final analysis were better off. When I used to work my way through school I used to say that it was good for you, that's a rationalization, it's not true. So if you say that I was better off for having had this illness and this setback, the reality is that I would be far better off not having had it. I could have been with my wife and children more, I could have been more productive, done more for society and for my family, had I not had this setback.

9

Wesley Martin, a 36-year-old man, began treatment seven years ago. His treatments have included hemodialysis, peritoneal dialysis and a kidney transplant.

Three days after Christmas in 1989, I was in emergency because my kidneys had failed, and my creatinine was over 1000 and I was struggling. So I did hemodialysis and stayed in emergency for three days. I was in and out of emergency several times. The hemodialysis did not seem to do too good for me, it was too hard on my heart, and after dialysis I was complaining that I was having a hard time breathing. There was one doctor who told me that I was drinking too much after dialysis, but I wasn't drinking too much at all, really I was drinking less. It was my heart, and that's why I was having a hard time. After two months on

dialysis, my doctor said that there was no way that I could go on with hemodialysis, so they put a catheter tube in my abdomen. That was done in February of 1990. Four days after my tube got blocked and I had to go back to surgery to have it fixed. I was in the hospital for about 10 days. This whole procedure was very painful. The CAPD nurse came to the house for the first time and set it all up and showed me how to do it.

If I had to go through the whole experience again I would take CAPD over hemodialysis any day. Even though you have to close the windows and turn the fan off, wash your hands for three minutes and clean your nails, the procedure itself is only 30 minutes. You just have to learn how to adapt. It's not a hard procedure, it's actually very easy.

When I changed from hemo to CAPD I was still on the heart and kidney transplant list, but while on CAPD my heart improved. When my heart got strong enough, I was put on the kidney transplant list. I only waited three weeks, because I have a rare type of blood, only four percent of the population has it, so it was only a matter of matching the tissue, which made it a lot easier. When I was put on the list, I knew that my time was coming, and it was lucky that I stayed home on that Saturday night. I was going to go out, but I stayed home and went to bed, and Sunday morning I got a call at 6:45. I was surprised, they told me not to eat, and not to worry or rush, but just to come down to the hospital. It was a sunny fall day on September 16th. When I arrived at the hospital I went up to the room that I was going to stay in after the surgery, and they prepared me for the surgery that was to come. I had a chest x-ray and then I went to the operating room, and the next thing I knew the lights went out at 11:15 a.m. and I woke up a 4:15 p.m. I don't remember too much from when I woke up. I was talking to my parents, I was alert, but I couldn't keep my eyes open, I was so tired, but I knew what was going on and I knew that everything turned out all right. I woke up, and was wide awake at 9:15 p.m., I had no pain at all. It was amazing.

You feel different once you have the transplant. When you come out of the hospital you do a little bit day by day, and you get back on your feet pretty fast. In the first days I was scared. Is the kidney all right? Am I getting a rejection? Do I have a fever? Is my urine all right? I worried if the kidney was going to work, or if it was going to reject. After time goes on you don't worry so much. I went back to work, that was the next step. At work it's the same thing, you worry about hitting yourself on the job. After some time you learn to adapt.

I had no problems at all with the employer or the employees, they even gave me a card and chocolate when I was in the hospital. I don't have much family here, just my mother and my father, but they were there for me at all times since the beginning of my illness. I couldn't ask for anything more.

One year and a half after the transplant I had a mild rejection. I was in the hospital for 10 days taking antirejection medication. That was worse than the operation, I think. You get headaches and you are sick to your stomach, you feel tired and feverish and weak. It was worth the price I paid to keep my organ. If I had to go through the whole procedure again, I would.

I learned to take life one day at a time, to enjoy nature, the sun and the birds. It has made me more nervous and stressful. I went through all these situations, and I don't want to go back down, I always want to stay up. I am now living a very good quality of life. I would like to give a very special thank you to the doctors that have treated me, and to the rest of the kidney and transplant staff, who helped me in the past and are still taking care of me today.

10

Moses Baker, a 76-year-old man, began hemodialysis 11 years ago.

More than 11 years ago, I started to notice the presence of some blood in my urine. After the initial blood and urine tests, the nephrologist told me that I had got a kidney infection, called nephritis, through a sore throat infection that I had at that time. I started to attend the nephrology clinic regularly. Two years after I started the treatment, the staff at the hospital told me that I had to start on dialysis and I did. I was uncertain when I started on dialysis because I did not know what to expect. But as the days went by, I found out that I made the right decision because dialysis did take away a big part of the suffering, the nausea and the depression, and I started to live a decent life again. The doctors put me on the list for a kidney transplant a couple of times but I took myself off that list because I would have to take very potent antirejection drugs and I was not ready to suffer anymore.

I was married to my second wife at the time I started dialysis, and my partner gave me a lot of courage and support. Sometimes I felt uncomfortable because my hands and feet swelled up, but once I was on the dialysis machine and the excess fluids were taken off of me, I felt much better. I follow the doctor's instructions as closely as I can because I realize that if I didn't do as they said, I am going to die, and I am not ready to die yet.

I also found courage in my four children and six grandchildren. I go visit three of my children in Toronto and in Ottawa and I have one daughter who lives here in Montréal. I receive a lot of support from my family and I believe that my family is the most important reason that keeps me wanting to live. I speak to my family nearly every day on the telephone long distance and I go to see them as much as I possibly can either by bus, by train or by plane.

On the days I do not come to the hospitals, I try to stay busy. I do my chores in the house and I go shopping for groceries. I try to keep in contact with friends and relatives.

For those people who have been unfortunate like me I have this to say to you, "Do not give up, have a lot of spirit and fight". There is a lot of struggle involved with hemodialysis. You are going to have good days and you are going to have bad days. If you obey the rules and regulations of the dietitians and the doctors as closely as you can, then you will see your life improving. I have had several surgeries after I started on dialysis including a double bypass surgery in which they put two metallic valves in my heart. They call me the bionic man. Being a strong fighter and having the will to live helped me cope with those surgeries and kept my heart ticking. I am 76 now; I figure if I keep watching myself as close as possible I may have another five to 10 years in my life. That would allow me to see my wonderful grandchildren grow up, and would also allow me to travel and do all the things I enjoy to do.

I see my story as one of hope and courage. If the information about myself and how I coped with my kidney failure helps other people, then maybe I'll see myself as a hero.

11

Sadie Golland, a 72-year-old woman, began hemodialysis three years ago.

I have been diabetic for a certain number of years, and I guess diabetes has caused my kidney failure. Before I started hemodialysis, I was very nauseous and I was not feeling too good, but after a certain length of time I started to feel better and most importantly, I am still alive.

Initially, when the doctor told me that I had to go on dialysis, I did not feel too good about it because I never heard anybody going on it, and I did not know what it was like. But after a few seminars in which the staff showed us the hemodialysis room and the hemodialysis machines, I became less apprehensive. I still don't know too much about the dialysis machine but I know that it's helping me. On the days of dialysis I feel a little tired. I usually lay down when I get home and have a little snooze, and when I get up I feel much better. I have no problem with the limitations on the diet, and I try to follow it as closely as I can. I try to forget about dialysis once I am not on it but deep down I am always thinking about it. I've got to remember to come to the dialysis three times a week and that makes it hard to forget about dialysis.

My family helped me a lot to cope with dialysis. My husband, my brother and my children have encouraged me a lot through my sickness, and I am grateful to them for their support. I have a housekeeper for now, who does all the work. I did a lot of work in my life so I guess it is time for me to relax. I am also thankful to the hemodialysis clinic staff because they have been wonderful to me.

Dialysis made a big difference in my life. I used to travel a lot but now I can't do that anymore. Actually two years ago, I went to Florida for three weeks thinking that everything will be all right. However I did not get the proper treatments there because they put me on the dialysis machine for only two hours when I am supposed to get three and a half hours. I became so sick and I came back to the hospital as soon as I could. My life is pretty different than what it was. I used to do a lot of work on my own, but now I realize that I get tired too fast especially after I finish dialysis. However the following day, I feel much better and I rely on that.

I suggest to people who have kidney problems to take dialysis because it's the best solution for their situation. Dialysis is a little tiresome because you sit around for almost four hours but it's your life and you can't fool around with that. The word dialysis sounds scary at the beginning. But once you start on hemodialysis, and you know what it means and how it works, your fear will no longer exist and you'll be thankful that such a machine exists. Dialysis will stay with you wherever you go and you better accept it and get on with your life.

12

Toby Williams, a 21-year-old man, began hemodialysis a year and a half ago. Following this interview, Toby had a kidney transplant.

I've been on dialysis for a year and a half now. At first, when I began dialysis, I was really upset. I had been on my way to playing college football in the United States, and all of a sudden I got sick. I couldn't believe this was happening to me, of all people. When I heard about the fistula I had to get, it just made everything worse. Then one day, my grandmother came to see me and she brought me her Bible from home. I started to read it, and it really calmed me down. It made me see things very differently. My grandmother recommended that I read the Book of Job, and I followed her advice. One sentence in particular from the Book of Job stayed with me: "The Lord giveth and the Lord taketh away". Since I'm very religious, reading the Bible has provided me with a lot of support.

Since I've started dialysis, some things have changed in my life. Before I began dialysis, I never used to think about illness or sick people, and being in a hospital has definitely changed that. Another aspect of my life that has undergone important modifications is my choice of diet. When I first came to the hospital, I had to see a special dietitian and she told me that there were all these foods I couldn't have anymore. Actually, about half of those were my favorite foods, and I'd eaten several of them that morning! Well, with time I learned how to deal with the problems that my dietary restrictions can create.

Actually, there have been some very positive things in my life since I started dialysis. One thing that's been good is that I always have fun when I come to the hospital for dialysis. The nurses are very nice, and the other people that are here are nice too. The atmosphere is really good, it's almost like a big family. Actually, since I started coming to the hospital, one thing in my life has become better than it was before I began dialysis. It started when I met Brian, another dialysis patient. Although he is several years older than I am, we get along really well. Often, I finish my treatment before he does, so I go over and speak to him. We talk and joke constantly, which sometimes drives the nurses up the wall. Before meet-

ing him, I used to be sort of shy, but now that's really changed. I'm much more comfortable around people now, especially women.

My friends have also been very supportive of the fact that I'm on dialysis, and that's been really important. They all accept me, and they don't treat me any differently than they did before. There's been no change in our relationships except that three times a week, I'm not there with them, and I can't eat all the same foods they do. But otherwise, I still play football, and spend time with all my friends on the football team.

One thing that's come up lately is the issue of a kidney transplant. I have been looking into it, but it's something I'm going to have to think about very carefully. The main reason for this is that the doctors have told me that if I get a kidney transplant, I won't be able to play football anymore. That's because football is a contact sport, and having a kidney transplant would prevent me from engaging in any contact sports. But right now, to deal with dialysis, I have a little secret. When I'm not in the hospital, I just don't think about dialysis. When I leave the hospital, I just continue my normal life. On a typical day, I hit the basketball court, work out, go home and watch some TV. I don't even think about dialysis at all. It takes a lot of discipline, but somehow I always manage to do it. When I do have to come in for treatments, I'm always in a good mood during the treatment, because if I were to be depressed, the treatment would just be that much harder. These days, it's very rare that I'm sad, or even mad. I don't know why I'm happy, it just happens. The way I see it, when you worry about something too much, you get grey hair. And I think I'm way too young to have grey hair.

13

A 68-year-old woman who wishes to remain anonymous began hemodialysis five months ago. Her story is told by her daughter.

We knew that my mother would have renal failure because two and a half years ago she had bypass surgery and we were told that renal failure may be one of the side effects. It was last summer when we noticed that she was deteriorating. Her kidneys were functioning less and less and the doctor proposed that she start dialysis. She was shocked when she found out. We came to visit the dialysis unit and she automatically thought that her life would be over. Because she's very strong, as she improved she started to accept it a little more and she began to feel encouraged. At the beginning, my dad wouldn't come to the dialysis unit because he wasn't really accepting it and he didn't want to show her that he was experiencing difficulty. Slowly, as he saw improvement in her, he began to come. Now he comes once a week. My father is very independent. He always helped around the house even if we're Italian!

I think the time it takes to do dialysis was the hardest part to accept and the fact that she can't travel anymore. It did affect us all in a way because it was an adjustment. My mother is an active woman and she likes to travel a lot and that stopped. She feels a lot better now that she's on dialysis, but I think she's a little bit depressed right now because she lost some of her hair because of the steroids she had to take. She always had a full head of hair. It is a little bit difficult. Although we tell her that it will grow back, I don't think she believes it.

You meet people here whose sibling for example has been on dialysis for a long time. They tell you their story and you compare notes and you start to feel better. It's like a support group. Coming here becomes a part of your life and you feel part of a family. My mother says that now she feels weak and before she was spunky but at least she laughs about it.

At the beginning, there are a battery of tests to go through. We met with the dietitian, the social worker and the psychiatrist. My mother thought that it was funny to meet with the psychiatrist because she wondered if dialysis would make her crazy! She didn't understand what his questions had to do with dialysis. So my sister and I spoke to the psychiatrist. At that time we were laughing so much maybe because we were tired. He probably thought that we were the ones who needed a psychiatrist!

14

Karen Smith, a 24-year-old woman, began treatment three years ago. Her treatments have included hemodialysis, peritoneal dialysis and a kidney transplant.

There was never an established reason why I got kidney disease, although I have a family history of lupus. I had never been told that I had lupus, but I was treated like I had a lupus-like condition. It only seemed to have one definitive flare-up, but my kidney function got lower and lower. I was 18 when I started to feel unwell. My kidney function started to fail, but it wasn't at a detectable range for me, it was only something that the doctors could see.

I started peritoneal dialysis when I was 21. I had a general concept of what it was when I started, but I didn't know anyone who had been on dialysis. The hospital that I started at gave me so much information about hemodialysis and peritoneal dialysis. They started to prep me when my creatinine reached 400, but I was told that I would not start until it reached 600. I had very close contact with one of my doctors, and he made things so much easier for me, just by doing things like making charts to show me what was going on with my creatinine. Even when I did start dialysis I was still so traumatized though. They said to me you are going to have dialysis today, in about 45 minutes actually, and that was quite a shock, even though I knew what it was going to be all about. Looking back now, in some ways I am glad that I was kind of naïve about it. I knew a lot of information about it, but you never really know how you are going to feel once you get on the machine, or doing it at home, or looking at how your lifestyle is going to change. It was definitely a time when I learned things about myself, my strengths and weaknesses, and my independence.

I think that by the time I could have started feeling badly about dialysis I had it down pat, so it never got to the point where I was really unhappy about it. But there were always certain times... like at one of my best friends' wedding. I was her maid of honor, and I had to leave the reception to go home to do a dialysis. Once you are given something like this, what's the alternative? If you don't do it, you will die. For me, anyway, it seemed like this was just the way things had to be.

I really liked the fact that I had the choice to do peritoneal dialysis, as opposed to hemodialysis. I really had a lot of problems with hemodialysis, because of my age, being in the hospital setting, some people on the machines look as if they are really sick, and I know that would have brought me down. I need to be independent. With peritoneal dialysis I could do it at home, and fit it into my lifestyle. I'm always on the go. I would take my bags with me to my friend's house and do a dialysis there, during trips I would do it in the car.

At least I could have a lifestyle with some resemblance to the one I wanted to have. I really tried not to let it hold me back. It was hard because I had to start with small steps. The first thing I did was go on an overnight trip, and then the second time I went away for a couple of days, and then I tried crossing the border, that seemed more risky psychologically, because if I screwed up there it would be more difficult for me to get help. Just setting small goals for myself, and then getting bigger and bigger. I lived in Atlanta for a summer, and at that point I felt like I could do anything on dialysis. It's kind of ironic, because it seemed as soon as I got to that stage, I had my transplant. I think it was a lesson for me that I needed to learn in life.

My family really supported me because of the past health history of my family. My mom died of lupus when my brother and I were small, so my dad was used to the hospital. My dad was very supportive, but I think that sometimes it was hard for him because of what he had gone through with my mom, and it almost seemed like a repeating cycle. My friends have been really helpful. They've been there for me for my dialysis and my pre-dialysis, and now that I've had my transplant. It's been good. I think that if I didn't have that network, it would be a lot more difficult for me. Having gone through a lot of stuff, you sort of tend to rely on your own strength a lot. I would say that there are times when everybody needs to lean on people, but when you look at the past and you see that you have battled big obstacles in your health history, sometimes you feel that you can go to yourself instead of going to somebody else, and that's really powerful. It feels really good. It's kind of weird to say, but sometimes I wonder what I would have been like if I hadn't gone through this experience. Although I would never want to go through it again, I am kind of glad that it happened. I feel that I have a lot of tools that will be helpful for the rest of my life.

I started off in Kingston, and there wasn't a problem with me going to university in the town that I grew up in. As soon as I started to push my boundaries I realized that Queen's University was not the be-all and end-all. I asked myself where I would like to live, and it was really Montréal. Coming here had more to do with Montréal than McGill, but it also meant a lot to me that I could get into a good university. There wasn't ever really a conflict with school. I found that especially at McGill they are so helpful with you. If you go and tell them that you may occasionally need help, they really make you feel that they'll support you. I didn't have to use it a lot because fortunately my dialysis went really smoothly, but if I had been sick, I know that there never would have been a problem with school, and that meant a lot to me. As far as my decision to be in school or not, dialysis really never held me back. A friend of mine also wanted to come and study in Montréal, so we got an apartment together.

I always went to school part-time. In my first semester I only took two courses, and from there on I always took three courses. With dialysis you really have to learn how to organize yourself, because you are doing it four times a day, and it forces you to be more organized than you normally would be. I found that the times when I had the most to do, I got the most done. There were definitely times when I felt overwhelmed and I had to drop courses for medical reasons. Last summer I was really tired because I was doing a lot of acting and taking a course at the same time. I was really burning the candle at both ends, and I had chronic exit site infections and was taking antibiotics. This combination was hard, so I had to drop a course, but when that happens, you just have to say, "What's more important, for me to look out for myself and make sure my health is managed, or the monetary value of the course, and missing out on the credits?" It teaches you not to be so hard on yourself.

I wasn't ready to have a transplant for a long time. In my mind I really had a problem with being that dependent on the antirejection medication for the rest of my life. It took me a while to decide that I wanted a transplant. Some people make that decision so automatically and I just don't understand how they can. I'm 24 years old, and I was thinking that this is likely not going to be the only transplant that I have, and if I am careful with it I can make it last for years, but I hope to live long enough to face the possibility that I may have to go through this all again. So I wanted to be completely ready to go through this for the first time, for it to be a positive experience, to be psychologically ready to deal with the drugs. I had a little bit of fear and uncertainty because it was a major operation and I have never had one before. The doctors say it's routine, and it may be routine to them, but not to me. Even after I had made the decision I wasn't so sure, and I did actually need that whole eight months in my head, walking around with my pager, waiting for it to go off, to deal with the idea that one time it will go off and I would go down to the hospital and get a transplant.

I was with my boyfriend, Freddie, we were having breakfast downtown, and my pager went off just before we got onto his motorcycle. He looked at the numbers and told me it was the hospital. I thought he was just joking. He actually dialed the number for the hospital because I couldn't, and I spoke to the CAPD secretary who had told me that I needed to come to the hospital. She said, "We have a kidney for you."

Just by coincidence my dad was coming from Kingston that day to meet me at the hospital where I had an appointment. It was such a coincidence, because my dad comes to visit me every three months, and for him to be coming that day when I got the call was just incredible. He was there which was great, and my boyfriend was there. One of my best friends, Zina, she was in Bermuda for the whole summer but she had come back the day before. It seemed like there were a lot of circumstances that were all coming into position to have this network for me to go through this. I had a lot of support.

I felt different in the recovery room, even though I felt the pain from after the surgery. I felt different in some way, not anything that I could put my finger on. I was really lucky that my kidney worked right off the bat. I feel really lucky that it went so well for me. I think that in some ways it had to do with the people I was surrounded with and the fact that I was really ready to have the transplant. I think that if I had just started dialysis and had a transplant right away, I would not have been in as good a position to deal with that type of traumatic event. After the first week or so that I got out of the hospital, following the transplant, I would sometimes be places and think, "Oh, I have to go home and do dialysis."

One area that was difficult for me, no matter how strong I was, was going through this ordeal at the certain age that I am. If you have a chronic illness as a child, you have the support of your parents to help you with regard to getting to appointments and decision-making. Similarly, as an older person, especially a married adult, you have the support of a spouse, who is there for you in a stable type of role. As a young independent person, many times when I need an intimate level of support, I feel quite alone. Even boyfriends and best friends can't always be there for you, because of the instabilities of young adulthood (building careers, school, other relationships, different levels of maturity, and so on).

The transplant gave me a lot of energy and this overwhelming feeling of productivity. You can equate it with having a particular job to do, and being told that there are 10 steps that you have to follow to do it, and then all of a sudden being told that now there are only three steps. I'm still going for the same goals, now it's just easier. I can concentrate on other things that will also better prepare me for those goals. That to me is great. It wasn't like I felt that my horizons opened up, it was just going to be easier to reach my goals.

15

Harry Goldner, a 77-year-old man, began hemodialysis four years ago.

The progression of the failure of my kidneys started in 1958. I had a case of gout. By February 1992, they quit on me at 2:00 in the morning. It was the most hideous feeling a person could have. Then I came on dialysis.

The first month on dialysis it was very difficult to adjust. You had to adjust your weight, your mental attitude, and eventually I developed an attitude, that this was going to be my life, and I am not going to be miserable, and I am going to be as compatible as I can. It was very hard on my wife who has been with me for so many years, but she also adapted, and we carried on. But we had to put in our minds, no more trips like we had before, no more dining-room meals like we had before. We were traveling representatives, my wife and myself, for over 45 years, we lived out of hotels, we lived in dining rooms of the hotels, and naturally it all had to come to an end.

So where do I go from here? Well, you develop an attitude about the hospital, where you come three times a week, it is your second home. It may sound foolish, because who wants to have a hospital as a home, but if you adopt the attitude that it is your second home, and you meet your nurses, who are the most kind and giving people, then you go on from there.

Now the dialysis that I was taking for the first couple of years was taking a lot out of me. My blood count was low, I needed a transfusion, and lo and behold along came a beautiful drug called "X". "X" to me is a wonder drug, and my doctor asked me if I would like to go on the study of this drug, and I consented immediately. To me, this is the most beautiful thing that has happened to me on dialysis. Why? Because at 6:30 or 6:00 every morning I am up and out of bed and I walk a mile and a half, double time, and then I come home, and I have my breakfast. This walk every morning is so successful that it has spruced up my muscles in my legs. Before I started my dialysis I used to walk, but during the time that my kidneys were failing I did not have the strength.

All of my life I have been a very independent individual, and I always said, "Well, if it's not good today, tomorrow will be a lot better." We had our disappointments, we had our good times, our bad times, so you have to take everything in stride, so when my kidney failure came up, I had to accept it and take it in stride.

A hero to me is someone who jumps into the river and saves a child, or something like that. Being a hero on dialysis and staying alive... maybe I can consider myself a hero. My wife always gives me support, my family gives me support. My friends always tell me, "My, you look wonderful!" I say, "Yeah, but I'm better off than you." They say, "Why?" "I am 77 years old, I get cleaned-out three times a week, you're in your 70's, and your kidneys are working 30, and 35 percent. See, so I'm better off than all of you." They look at me and think that I have lost my marbles, but that's the truth! So if you want to consider me a hero, I will accept your consideration.

16

Andor Lekay, an 88-year-old man, began hemodialysis seven months ago.

After several blood and urine tests, my doctor told me that one of my kidneys was 50-percent working and that the other kidney had stopped functioning. It took me about three months before I started on dialysis because I had to have a fistula placed in my arm. Unfortunately the veins in my arm were not strong enough and the doctors finally placed a catheter in my chest area and that's how I have been doing my dialysis until this day.

When the doctors told me that I had to be on dialysis, I did not know I had to come three times a week. I thought that maybe I would have to come only once a week. I can't do anything during these three days but what can I do? It's either dialysis three times a week or my life. Actually I don't mind dying, but my wife who is 12 years younger than me does, and that is the reason why I took dialysis.

Now I know that I have to take this treatment for the rest of my life and I accept it. Everybody else who is having dialysis comes three times a week so why should I complain? I am a realistic person and I know that at my age things like this happen.

I don't think too much about dialysis and I try to keep busy by reading, listening to music or having a half-an-hour walk every day around my building when the road is not slippery. I have a few friends who call me at home and discuss their family life with me. All my life I was an architect. Actually I was one of the architects who designed the Ross Pavilion of the Royal Victoria Hospital. I always designed and always kept myself organized. Dialysis was another way of organizing myself and maybe that was the reason why I handle it well.

Dialysis is a little bit hard during the first two months but after a while you get used to it. When you take dialysis you should know what to expect. In order for you to stay alive you have to take this treatment and not waste your energy fighting it. The results of dialysis will depend on the person who is taking it. I can't force dialysis on someone who does not want it but I can tell them that dialysis is the only way to stay alive. That's all.

17

A 43-year-old man who wishes to remain anonymous began treatment 20 years ago. His treatments have been hemodialysis and a kidney transplant.

I've been on dialysis for 20 years. I began my journey at about age 22 or 23. At that time I was still in university and how I found out was that one time I went to urinate and it was a dark color. Before this I had also had some experiences where I was very tired a lot of the time. So I decided to go to a doctor and he found that I had high blood pressure. I went to a specialist and he put me in the hospital. While I was in the hospital, they did some tests to discover why a young person of 22, 23 would have high blood pressure. All they could figure out was that the high blood pressure damaged the kidneys and when the kidneys get more damaged you get more high blood pressure and it's like a cycle.

I remember that I was at the hospital and I had a young intern who didn't know anything about dialysis and he told me that I was going to have to be hooked up to a machine for the rest of my life. No explanations, nothing, just being on a machine for the rest of my life is what I thought. That night in the hospital I really cried, I cried my eyes out. What was going to happen to me? At that time I was a young kid and you think that you are invincible at that age. After a while, the doctor that I was associated with explained in more detail what was happening. So from the initial shock, it wasn't too bad. He explained that I would only have to come in once in a while, versus being hooked up to a machine all the time. Even with the more realistic information it's still a trauma in your life.

I have the type of family, I'm talking brothers and sisters, who are afraid of diseases. They like to stay away from it. They don't like to talk about it. I had a girlfriend at that time and she was a nurse. So she understood more and so she got me through. She got me through it by really reminding me all the time that life wasn't over and that I still had a lot to contribute and to give and to do. She used to say that if someone throws you a curve you get out of the way, you don't let it hit you in the face.

I was on dialysis for about eight to 10 years, I don't remember exactly. Then I got a transplant and I had that for about three years until I came back to dialysis. Before you start dialysis, the doctors postpone it a little bit, but if you postpone it too long, you get too sick. Once you start, the first treatment or the first few weeks are difficult I guess, but after that you start feeling well again. Dialysis is here to help you, its like a hate and love relationship. You have to rush here and you hate that but then you realize that if you didn't have it, you wouldn't be here. It's that kind of relationship.

The first five years, I was teaching and I was able to carry on my work but after a while it got to be too hard because I'd go in the morning and finish let's say 4:00 or 4:30. Then I would rush to dialysis and I had to do my own set-up. So I'd get on about 5:00, 5:30 and it takes about four hours so by the time I'd get home it would be around 11:00 and I would have to be up early in the morning. So I decided to stop teaching and now I do some stained glass and I have a little catalogue business and a dog at home to keep me busy.

If you look at this situation, the alternative is death so I don't really think you could consider me a hero. You see, if death scares you more than this, and this is the alternative to death then you can't really consider yourself a hero. On the other hand, you can look at the quality of your life. You see, if you still go out and have a social life, then that is coping. So I guess, I have coped well. I know people who complain that they can't drink and they can't eat so they don't go out. Well, the drinking and eating are not the only things you are living for. You go out, you drink a bit, you eat a bit, and you socialize or just eat a little less during the day.

To somebody who is thinking, this is it, this is the end of it, there is nothing else, I would tell them from my experience that it is not the end. During my years on dialysis I have travelled to the Philippines, Japan and Hawaii all on the same trip. It can be done. You just have to arrange it with the hospitals there. There are also the financial concerns, especially for the breadwinner of the family. It is a real concern because dialysis is very time-consuming and working also really depends on how you are feeling.

Sometimes when you have something thrown at you and you survive, you become stronger. Now, I am more understanding and I don't get as mad, it has shaped my character for the better. For disappointments, I say, "well yes, I can't do it but there will be another time". I don't react like this all the time obviously but the majority of the time this is how I look at things. I think that you begin to accept life as it is, knowing that it is up and down and knowing that if it is worse now, it will get better.

Basically if I was a young patient starting on dialysis I would want to know if my life was over and you know, it isn't, it is far from it. My life is satisfying. I'm still amazed, not having kidneys, they are relatively important organs in your body, not indispensable obviously, but you have this dialysis machine and if you follow your diet and you are relatively active, you can go on. Everything has a cost in life, even more so when you are sick but you continue, you go on and that's the way it is. In life, your imagination is your limit, for everyone out there, even people who don't have a disease.

18

Maria Franco, a 40-year-old woman, began treatment eight years ago. Her treatments have included hemodialysis and peritoneal dialysis.

I've been on dialysis for eight years now. At the beginning, I was on hemodialysis, but eventually I switched to peritoneal dialysis. The reason I switched was that I had a small baby at home, and I didn't want to go in to the hospital all the time.

When I first began dialysis, I was scared and I didn't want to go through with the necessary operation. But after I had the operation and I actually started dialysis, I got used to it.

Several things have helped to make my situation easier. I have my mother, and she comes over a lot. Also, my son comes home for lunch every day. My husband helps, everyone helps. Of course I get worried sometimes, but I don't let it bother me. I know I'm on dialysis, but I accept it. I just think that this is the way my life is, and what else can I do? I could be upset that I'm on dialysis, but if I was to let myself down, what kind of life would I have? How would I keep going? This way, I get along.

It has been all right to raise my son while on dialysis because I have scheduled my life. In the morning, I usually get up and do my dialysis treatment first. Then I get ready, have a coffee, and wake my son up to get him ready for school. I bring him to school and then I do whatever else I have to do. Afterwards, I go pick him up again. I go on vacation, and that's no problem as long as I keep my schedule of treatments. I can also go out at night, I just have to schedule my dialysis. In that way, peritoneal dialysis has been very convenient. I can always fit in my treatments when my son is in school or when I'm not busy.

Nothing has changed in my life. I still do everything I need to do, because my treatments don't take very long. Since I don't work, I've had time to get involved in a lot of activities. I'm a leader in my son's clubs once a week at his school, and we bring the kids to many interesting places. The only time I couldn't go along was when they went camping, since it was too complicated to work out my treatments. I also go to school myself once a week, I volunteer at the library, and I teach kids catechism to prepare them for Communion.

It's true that in the beginning, my situation was very hard, and I didn't want to accept it. But my son gave me a lot of courage, because I knew that he needed me. Eventually, after I got through the operation, I was able to better accept the situation. When the doctors discuss kidney transplants with me, I'm not sure about it because I think I'm doing well now. Dialysis is definitely a big part of my life, and it's something that I have to do every day. But it doesn't stop my life, and I see it as just one other thing I have to do.

19

Eleanor Hinton, a 58-year-old woman, began hemodialysis five weeks ago.

Not long ago I went to see my primary doctor because I was suffering from constipation. My practitioner told me that my kidneys had failed and mentioned something about dialysis. The doctor also told me that my heart had became enlarged and that I should start dialysis otherwise I would drop dead. I had no other choice but to accept that treatment. The doctors wanted to put my name on the list for kidney transplant. I refused because I am a realistic person, and I thought that a younger person could benefit from it more than I would.

I was a little bit upset when the doctor told me that my kidneys had failed because I was still young and I have five grandchildren that I want to see grow up. Hemodialysis was scary at the beginning because of those needles in my arm and those tubes that were coming out of me. However, after a while I started to get used to it. On the days of dialysis, I don't feel like doing anything. I just want to go home and lay down in my bed for a couple of hours. The limitations on the diet and the liquids bother me a lot. I'd love to have more water but I can't have it because the doctor said that it may give me a heart attack. Laying on the bed for four hours during dialysis is very tough and I am starting to have backaches lately. I get up in the morning and I am still alive and I should feel fortunate that this hemodialysis machine exists.

Hemodialysis has made a big difference in my life. I can't go to see my daughters anytime I want to because I have to ask for permission from my driver. And when I go there I can only stay overnight because I have to come back the next day for my dialysis. I don't feel I am my own boss anymore. My grandchildren often ask me why I didn't play with them anymore. I tell them that I am tired and do not feel like playing with them. Hopefully someday when I get better I'll be able to play a little more with them. I enjoy smoking cigarettes but the doctor cautioned me against cigarettes because my health may deteriorate. I told him that I was going to die anyway so I might as well smoke a cigarette and enjoy it. I still smoke but I do it less.

My two daughters and my two sons are doing all they can to support me. They come to see me now and then but they've got their own kids and that keeps them pretty busy. Right now I am living with my cousin and she does the cooking and the cleaning around the house. I always had courage and whenever I had a problem I always sat down, looked at my problem first and worked it out. I always believed that whatever will be will be. I try to keep my spirits up by doing a lot of reading and watching a little bit of television.

Take dialysis and look up to the higher authority because that helps sometimes. Accept dialysis because you have no other choice. Do as you are told to do. Rely on yourself and be strong because nobody else will help you through dialysis but yourself. Your life changes when you are on dialysis but it does not have to change for the worse.

20

Ayad Kolta, a 62-year-old man, began treatment four years ago.
His treatments have consisted of hemodialysis and a kidney transplant.

In 1978, I had a heart attack. When I was hospitalized, the doctor told me that one of my kidneys had stopped functioning. Between the period of 1982 to 1987, my other kidney failed and my name was put on the waiting list for a kidney transplant. In February of 1989, I received a kidney transplant and everything seemed to be going well until February of 1992 when the transplanted kidney failed. The only solution to my problem then was to start hemodialysis, otherwise I would die. In the meantime my name was put again on the waiting list for another kidney transplant and I am still waiting till this day for that kidney.

When the doctor told me that my kidney failed, I accepted the news and went on with my life. Hemodialysis was inconvenient because I had to come to the hospital three times a week. On the days of dialysis, I am usually in a bad mood and try to avoid speaking to anyone. Once the dialysis is finished, I am very weak and go straight to bed in my house. When I get up and have my meal I feel fine. The other inconvenience about hemodialysis is that I have to watch my liquid and salt intake. However, except for the three days of hemodialysis, I feel fine the rest of the week. My wife and my children give me all the help they can give and that's very important in these situations.

When I had a kidney transplant, I was less tied to the hospital and I could do whatever I wanted. However, many things went wrong with that transplant. I started developing high blood pressure, high blood sugar and I soon started having problems with my eyesight. I was also taking many antirejection drugs and that might have caused the symptoms that I developed. So if you take these things into consideration, the kidney transplant and hemodialysis balance out because they both have their conveniences and inconveniences.

For those people who have just been diagnosed with kidney failure, the best way to go about it is to accept it, and try to live a normal life with whatever means you have. In my case, believing in God was very helpful because it helped me accept my situation as part of my destiny.

21

Janice Anthony, a 43-year-old woman, began hemodialysis one year ago.

In 1988 when I started to do my papers here to get my permanent residence I went for my medical and they found out that I had diabetes. They started treating me for the diabetes but I wasn't really taking good care of myself, I wasn't really taking the tablets that I should. In 1994, because I had to buy all my medication on my own and I was all alone and I had my four children that I had to support, I couldn't buy the medication that I wanted so then it got out of control.

They told me the kidney problem happened because of the diabetes and because I didn't take care. Always I'm sick, and finally in August the doctor called me and told me that he was going to put me on dialysis. They did all the tests on me and finally they put me on. My first time on dialysis I cried. I cried so much, I sat here when I was waiting, I cried, I cried, I cried so much I couldn't understand. I was looking at everybody here and saying what is going on, I don't understand how I'm going to be hooked to a machine for four hours. I cried the whole evening through.

At the beginning I still was feeling sick and weak but now, it is a whole different story, I'm telling you. I feel more strong. You should have seen me when I first came here, I couldn't even walk and now I can run to catch the bus. I can't even believe it. I used to just stay at home and come to the hospital by taxi but now it is a big difference. I can do anything that I used to do before. I do my housework, I cook, I go do my shopping but I can't carry too much because I have the fistula in my arm. But I go, I walk, I do everything I am supposed to be doing, I am a 100 percent better than when I started.

The only hope is dialysis, and I think it's really working. It worked for me. It really helped me a lot so I would encourage anybody to go on dialysis. I am a hero because I fought and encouraged myself. My family was very courageous also, especially my son. All my children are here now, I have a 19-year-old son who is very supportive, he gives me all the hope. He says, "Mommy you have to live, you have to live to see me finish my school." He says, "You are going to live to see me finish my career and I am going to buy you a car." He will sit with me and ask me so many questions about my sickness. He gives me more courage because I am happy for him and he is happy for me. He wants to go to college, I know he will make it, I did. For me, I am a Christian, I believe in God, and a lot of hope. I believe God was there with me to help me because I was there by myself and I know that all along He was there while I encouraged myself. I knew that I had to make it because I am the only one that my kids have; even though their father is there, he is not the person they were looking for. He was not there for a long time and what they expected they didn't get, so then they are looking to me. I have to live. I have to make it. It is a fight to make it, believe me.

A lot of things changed, my lifestyle changed but I am still the same. I can do everything because of the dialysis and because of the strength and the hope that everything is going to be okay. At first I know that everybody is going to be scared because you don't know what you have to go through, but I am telling you that there is hope.

22

Liberato Quieti, a 51-year-old man, began treatment three years ago. His treatment has included peritoneal dialysis and hemodialysis.

I went for a routine check up in 1992 at the hospital, and the doctor found out about my kidney problem, but at that time it was very advanced. I was told that I had to go on dialysis. I had the option of waiting, but I would have to be on a very strict diet. I decided to go on dialysis right away. This was to my advantage because there was no damage done to any of my other organs. When I started I had two choices about what type of dialysis to be on, CAPD, which is done at home, or hemodialysis. I tried CAPD for a year and a half, but I had two infections, so I decided to go onto hemodialysis. The catheter was removed and now it's my turn on hemodialysis.

The treatment is going well, and I have no other medical problems. I could not get a transplant earlier because I had my catheter removed and I had some stones in my gall bladder removed, but I am on the transplant list now, and I am looking forward to that.

It changed my lifestyle a bit. It restricted my capacity to work. I am attached to the hospital, and it takes away some of my freedom to travel and to do whatever I want. It affects me a bit socially as well. I can't always join my friends the way I used to. The doctors and nurses do their best. The rest depends on the patient, how you survive it and how you fight it. Me personally, I don't let the disease control me, I control the disease. I do the best with whatever health I have left.

What I would want from people is for them to understand what I am going through and nothing more. You need people that respect you and don't demean you.

I would advise new patients to be active. Don't think about the disease, make plans, have a hobby, have dreams to keep you going. It is very important to have a dream, to do something with your life, especially if you are young. You need to plan, something so that you don't reach a dead end, so in this respect a dream is very important.

For anyone that goes on dialysis they should not think of themselves as sick, their kidney is sick, not them. Maintaining your diet, controlling fluids and getting rest are very important, just as important as dialysis. You have to be your own doctor sometimes and help yourself.

For those of you who cannot be transplanted for one reason or another, you should not lose hope. In the future, with all the research, some new and more effective treatment will be available and life will become a lot better.

23

Remedios Salvo Roxas, a 72-year-old woman, began treatment seven years ago. Her treatments have been hemodialysis and peritoneal dialysis.

I have been on dialysis for about seven years. In 1982, I was feeling like I was hitting a wall. I had backaches, heartaches, stomach cramps, and I was feeling cold like a dead person. I was in heavy pain in general. My daughter is a nurse, and who lives with me, took me to the hospital. The doctor found out that I had high blood pressure and referred me to the department of internal medicine. After a whole year of blood tests, a biopsy, and check-ups, the doctors told me that I was suffering from kidney failure.

When the doctor told me that I had to start on dialysis, I did not object and followed his orders. I would have preferred that I was not sick but what could I have done? One thing I am certain about, is that I am glad I have the chance to be on dialysis, because if I had been in my country, I'd be gone a long time ago because medicine, doctors, and procedures such as hemodialysis are out of my reach. As long as dialysis keeps me alive and I am able to have a decent life, I won't ask for more. My daughter has taken care of me since day one on dialysis. She cooks my meals, brings me to the hospital and provides me with all kinds of support. Unlike what I have seen with the rest of the patients, who have been sort of neglected by their own children, my daughter has made my well-being as her top priority. She cares about me and she does for me what, me her mother, is supposed to do for her. There is not a single thing that I want to do that she would let me do it alone. She is worried about me and she prefers to go with me wherever I go even for a little errand. When I ask her why she was doing that for me, she replies, "Why, are you tired of me?" Some friends of ours have become jealous for the support I receive from my daughter.

To those people who are about to embark on dialysis, try to be patient and follow what the doctor and the dietitian say. As long as you follow the rules of the game, you will be all right. Whether you want it or not, dialysis is still the option for your situation and you better accept it and consider yourself lucky you are able to have it. You won't be able to do all the things you used to do before but you will still be alive and that's all that counts.

24

Luigi Larosa, a 67-year-old man, began hemodialysis four and a half years ago.

During the winter of 1992, while I was working at my barber shop, I started to feel weak and sick. After the initial blood and urine tests, I was referred to the Royal Victoria Hospital because my doctor suspected that I may have some problems with my kidneys. Another set of blood and urine tests at the hospital revealed that both of my kidneys had failed. The doctor urged me to start dialysis right away. Initially he stuck a tube in my belly and started me on peritoneal dialysis. A fistula was inserted in my left arm and a month later I started hemodialysis treatment. My name was also put on the waiting list for a kidney transplant.

When I first was told that my kidneys had failed, I could not believe this news and tried to deny what was happening to me. However the doctor told me that there was no other way out and that I should start dialysis right away. The doctor added that dialysis was a must otherwise my internal organs would be filled with water and I would die.

The initial days were very tough for me because hemodialysis put many restrictions on my lifestyle. On one hand I was tied to the hospital three times a week and I could not do much after I was done with dialysis. Once I got home after dialysis, I felt very tired and could only lay in my bed and sleep. On the other hand I could not eat or drink the things that I used to eat before I started dialysis. Us Italians like to eat tropical fruits, vegetables, and drink wine. However, with the new limitations on my diet I couldn't have anything that had a lot of potassium. However, thanks to dialysis I am still alive and have been able to survive four and a half extra years. I should also feel lucky because in poor countries, people cannot afford to have a dialysis machine and usually die soon after they start to have kidney problems.

I am always hoping that some day I will be able to receive a kidney transplant because that would eliminate the needles in my arm and I would not need to come to the hospital three times a week. A kidney transplant would also eliminate the restrictions on my diet and I would be able to eat and drink properly. I have seen many patients who felt so good and rejuvenated when they received a kidney transplant. However, some of them did not make it very far because their body did not accept all the antirejection drugs.

For those people who have just been diagnosed with kidney problems, I advise you to follow the doctor's orders properly and to stick to the diet rules. Dialysis will stay with you throughout your life and you will have to get used to it. The most important thing however is that you should not let dialysis affect you mentally. For that you have to be strong and accept things good or bad as they come.

25

Mrs. Deneka, an 81-year-old woman, began hemodialysis four years ago.

When I started dialysis four years ago it worked quickly because I had only one kidney left that wasn't functioning very well. My other kidney had been removed when I was only 23 years old. Before I knew what was happening I began to hear voices in my head, saying "You are going to die, you are going to die!" and so I prayed that I would die at home and not on the street. One day my mother said to me that when I saw the doctor I should tell him about hearing the voices because maybe something was causing that. I saw the doctor, he examined me and asked if I hurt anywhere and I told him that I had very severe backache. It was then he told me that he believed there was something wrong with my kidneys. He did some more tests and told me to go home and rest. When my condition didn't improve he put me in the hospital and that was when the operation to remove my kidney was performed. Afterwards he told me that if I hadn't had the operation I would not have survived, that I had been on the brink of death.

Now I am an 81-year-old and my second kidney was not working well and so I was put on hemodialysis treatments three times a week. I take life as it comes for as long as I will live. The doctor says I will live to be 140 years old because I look after my health.

Right now I am living with my daughter who is very good to me. She always makes sure that I am very clean, without the smallest spot. I myself believe it's important for a person to be clean. My daughter is also very attentive about my food and takes great pains to see that I eat well.

Dialysis has changed many things in my life. Now, I don't go out anywhere and I don't even go shopping. The stores are crowded with people and germs, and since people like us are very susceptible to germs, I avoid crowds and enclosed places. The doctor has advised me not to go to the stores in winter. In fact, I am also asthmatic and some people have the flu in winter so I could easily catch pneumonia, which I already have had three times. That is why I have to be very careful about that and about my general health. Aside from that, I believe that dialysis is something that prolongs one's life. It's a good invention, whoever invented it. Above all, it's good for those who still have some strength and for someone like me who is still clear-headed. In fact my doctor says that even my voice is not that of an old person and that I don't sound like an 81-year-old woman.

It's been almost four years since I started on dialysis, yet it's gone by very quickly. At the beginning I knew nothing about it, but I visited the dialysis clinic and I saw people sitting there quietly. It took me quite a while to adapt and I'm only just beginning to get used to it. It's not exactly fun but you do meet a lot of nice people here. There's one man who always helps me when I'm having trouble walking. In any case, I like to talk and so I speak to everyone. They call me "Madame Angel" because I collect angels that you can pin on your clothes and I give them to many of the people here. Apropos of that, I was the seventh born in my family, the seventh daughter and I'm reputed to have a gift from God, although I don't know exactly what that gift is. Apparently, when I was young I cured an aunt who was paralyzed and she was able to walk again. A Monsignor told me that I had God's gift. Maybe it's because I am a good person and I am not mean to others.

When I can't sleep and wake up in the middle of the night, I pray for everyone, for all those people I see at the hospital, they are all in my prayers. I know they haven't the time for prayer because they are younger than me so I ask the angels to look after them and their children. When things don't go too well, I speak to God and I ask him to get going up there. I ask Him to look in His book to see if He can't find something in there to improve our lot.

26

Gérard Martineau, a 74-year-old man, began hemodialysis five months ago.

I went to see my doctor, who has been treating me for quite a while. He said that I needed an operation because I had cancer of the lung. They removed the cancer from the top left portion of my lung. Just before the operation, the doctor said that they could not operate because the kidneys were too weak. I passed another test for the kidneys, but they collapsed, so I have no kidneys left. The doctor that looked after my kidneys said that I should get dialysis.

So that's the story—now I have to live with dialysis, which I don't like, but I have to. It's only from July, but it will stay for the rest of my life. It's a disturbance in my life. I live with my wife, and we live very good. Now I have to go three days a week for treatments of three and a half hours each, so there is a big difference in my life.

When they told me that I had to go on dialysis, I had no idea of what it was. It was a shock to me. I learned about dialysis when I came here. While I'm on dialysis I usually fall asleep, or I look around. Sometimes it's long, but other times it goes quick.

The lady who takes care of the food came to see me today, she restricts me quite a bit, but what can you do? Now I have to start eating the right things, because now I have a diet and I have to follow it. While I'm in the hospital they feed me, they feed me a lot.

For new patients I would advise that you get your kidneys checked way before. I did have check-ups, but it was unfortunate that mine collapsed all at once. The doctor told me, "From one month to the other, they were down to nothing."

27

Hanna Sahinovic, a 42-year-old woman, began treatment 10 years ago. Her treatments have consisted of peritoneal dialysis, hemodialysis and two kidney transplants.

I have been on and off hemodialysis for 10 years. When I first got sick they put me on peritoneal dialysis but I got an infection and I started hemodialysis. I have had two kidney transplants. The first one was in 1990 and my body rejected it after two and a half years. I was very depressed. I didn't want to see my family. It was terrible but after a while when I came back here for dialysis everybody gave me morale to live and so did my family and friends at home. The last kidney transplant I had was in 1995 and I developed a viral infection one week later and lost the kidney. I was in the hospital for almost three months because they thought that the kidney was not being rejected, that the kidney was still good and that it would start working. I am willing to go for a kidney transplant a third time. The surgery is not that bad. The first day you feel a little bit sick but now they have all sorts of medication which help so it's nothing to be really afraid about.

Being on dialysis helps me a lot and I am sure that if it were not for dialysis I would be dead by now. Before dialysis I could not even drink a sip of water without vomiting. I could not walk because my legs were all swollen. My husband had to carry me to the bathroom. Before dialysis my life was really miserable. Now I think I have a normal life. I can't drink a lot but I am very lucky because I don't have any problems with my potassium and calcium like some patients. I don't know why it's this way but maybe my system is better. I can eat normally but

they said not to eat chocolate but the secret is out and I do eat chocolate once in a while without any problem. I like to go shopping, cook and clean, read and do crochet. I also like to go up to the country in the Laurentians.

My family and friends are a source of great support. My husband helps me a lot. My daughter was only six years old when I got sick. I brought my sister-in-law from Poland because I knew one day that I would have to go to the hospital for longer term, not only overnight. My husband was busy in the restaurant and he didn't have too much time to help me so I brought my sister-in-law and she took care of my daughter and she liked her so I didn't have a problem with that. They came every day to visit me. My daughter understands things now but when I was to get a kidney in 1990 she was 10 years old and she threw herself on the floor and she was crying for me not to go because she was thinking that I was going to die because everybody thinks that sometimes after surgery you don't get up. Now she sees that when I go for surgery I come back. She sees that it's not that bad.

The advice I would like to give to new patients is to not be afraid of the machines because they are not that bad. Liver and heart patients have more to fear about their lives than kidney patients. Kidney patients have choices. We can come to the hospital several times a week for a few hours and then we are free to go home and do anything we want or we can choose to do peritoneal dialysis at home. I lead a normal life and I continue doing the things I like. I take it easy on the days when I come in for dialysis.

28

Mary Makaros, a 75-year-old woman, began hemodialysis 10 years ago.

I wasn't feeling well for a long time and I was always tired and it wasn't like me because I was very energetic. I would go to work and two hours later I was very tired. I went to see my boss and I told him I don't know what is wrong with me, I can't figure it out. So he said, "Okay go home". So I go home and I rest and rest until the next morning when I went back to work. Again I was down. I went and saw the boss—and I go home again. The boss said, "Listen, would you just stay home a couple of weeks until you get better". He didn't know it was anything and neither did I; he thought it was the flu or something. This went on for a couple of months until I said to myself that it wasn't normal. I am going to see what is wrong. So I went and found a doctor. So after so many tests they found out that one of the kidneys had shrunk and that is when they knew that it was kidney problems I had. So from then on they told me that I was going to have to do dialysis. I said, "No way, I am not going on dialysis". So I went back to him and he said, "Look, you have about four more weeks to live, either you do it or..."

Well now I am on dialysis. What I do like about it is that they serve me breakfast in bed. I feel a lot better now that I am on dialysis but I also get very sick on dialysis. I throw up a lot and my pressure goes down.

I waited to the very end, until I was almost crawling on the floor, not knowing that it was caused by the kidney problem. They said I only had four weeks left. I wouldn't have said that I had only four more weeks, but I would tell people that if you have to have it then go and get it. Nobody likes it at first, it ties you down and you can't do what you want to do. I used to travel and I can still do that. It takes a lot of courage to do this. I have been here for 10 years and some people have been here 15 years. One lady was here, she passed away last year but she was on dialysis for 22 years and she was a young woman too and she had three transplants and that is what is called courage you know.

I try to live a life as normal as I can. There are some things I can't do, hard work like painting the house, I can't do. I still go out a lot, I do all my housework and shopping and if I don't feel like doing it one day, I'll do it the next day. Don't get me wrong, it is still pretty bad, not everything is good, I had to give up my job and stuff. It is funny because it is 10 years now and I remember the doctor told me that it was only going to be a couple of times.

The nurses and doctors are very good here. They are like family. I think that they have to have special training for us. They have to be very patient with us. Only with all of this can I live, and so it is like a gift.

29

A woman who wishes to remain anonymous began hemodialysis two years ago.

It was really bad at first. When I found out, I was sure it was a mistake, because I'm healthy, there's no disease in my family, on either side, so I just couldn't figure it out, you know. Anyhow, I found it very, very hard, because I smoke, I like tea and coffee, and I love to go out in the evenings. I have a drink, not alcohol, but socialize, you know, and this you have to be very careful about. So, it cuts your legs right out from under you. I had just retired and I didn't have any retirement funds, you know, people retire and they go someplace and do something. I didn't have that, so everything was just nil. At first it's a terrible feeling because you are sick to your stomach all the time and you're taking medicine and trying to cope with it, and you're always sick. People say, "Why don't you put in for a kidney?" No, kidneys are a lot of problems, and I could never take a kidney and it not agree with me, and then be put back on dialysis. No, I'd get a gun and shoot myself.

I am my own cushion. I help myself, it's nobody else. I hear some-body else's sad story, like if they say they're going to meetings with the others, I don't want to hear about your sickness. I am sick and please keep your sickness to yourself. You're not interested in mine and I am not interested in yours. That's the way I look at it.

I have courage, but I am not much of a hero. My family gives me my courage. I bought a house with my daughter when I went to retire. I invested my money in the house with her, so I have this beautiful home. All my daughters support me, they talk with me, if I want to go shopping, or if I want to go somewhere they help me out.

I don't go to church anymore, because I don't want to put myself out. I put myself out all my life, I worked, I've raised my girls, now it's time for me and I've got this... forget it. I take care of myself and that's it.

Some people can accept sickness altogether different. When I was raised, my father was British, my mother Irish. Now, British people, around my father's age group, when they get married they want you to marry someone healthy, good hair, good teeth, this is the British way of think-ing. When I was about eight or nine I had to get glasses, because I was short-sighted, my father couldn't get over it. He said to my mother there's some flaw in your family. Just because my family was like that, it doesn't mean I am.

I never tell anyone I am on dialysis. I am too embarrassed. It's a disease, I don't like it.

I would tell new patients to try and do what they like. Just take an interest in something that you like, that's what I would tell them. Try and look at the happiness of things, look at the happy parts, even something like the TV, this is the only way. I like to sew. I make aprons or dish towels, very plain things, you know. If I could word it right, for people that are starting, especially if they are intelligent, now that's more so, they should continue school. You don't want to be a leech on anyone else, don't be a problem, to your mother, your father, your sister, or brother, try and get a grant from the government yourself. You do all the work. Yes, definitely, I'm all for that, yes that's what I would do if I was young.

30

René Ricard, a 71-year-old man, began hemodialysis two years ago.

At the beginning, I started my dialysis treatments by having a fistula put into my arm. However, I thought that having several injections [needlings] a week was tough. I thought that if I had a catheter in my chest, I wouldn't have to worry about that. At the beginning, I was getting those needles in the arm all the time, and it didn't suit me at all. Sometimes, the injections [needlings] would not work, and they had to be done over several times. That was really painful for me, and I didn't like having to go through that.

Eventually, my fistula was switched for a catheter in my chest, and now I am a lot more satisfied. There is a lot less pain involved in dialysis for me now because of this change.

Actually, even with a catheter it is not certain that setting up will work right away. Sometimes the tube is dirty, so the nurses have to start over. However, that doesn't involve any pain for me, so I don't mind that. When I had the fistula, I found that a situation like that involved a lot more pain. If I were to speak to anyone who is currently receiving injections [needlings], I would recommend switching to a catheter if possible, because it reduces the amount of pain involved. Now, I am very satisfied with my dialysis treatment. I only wish that I had switched methods sooner.

The main thing which has changed since I started dialysis is that now my chest feels very numb, and I can't feel anything if I touch it. Since I now have a catheter, I also have to be very careful about coming into contact with water. Otherwise, I don't mind coming to dialysis three times a week. I don't suffer anymore, so now everything is perfect.

31

Antonio Batista, a 57-year-old man, began treatment 25 years ago. His treatments have been hemodialysis, peritoneal dialysis and a kidney transplant.

In my case it's a long story. You see, in 1971 I had a transplant right away without dialysis. I didn't know what was dialysis. I heard from some people who were on dialysis at that time that it was very hard, because in '71 they did not have certain kinds of machines. My transplant, I had it from one of my sisters, you know, it was okay right away, and it worked for almost 20 years. It was very good, and after 20 years I had a very

normal life, no problems. When I started to see that the kidney was finished you know, I was a little worried, because I was taking dialysis three times a week, you know, so I had to do it. It was very difficult when I started and that is why I started chronic ambulatory peritoneal dialysis, because I was working and I was more free, you know, and with the business, it gave me more time to take care of the business. But after an infection with CAPD I had to come to hemodialysis, because I did not have any choice.

Dialysis changed my life, sure, I am not free anymore, I have to come here three times a week. I still live my life, a little different than before, but I do my things, you know. I like being in self-care. Self-care in a way, is the better way to do it, because you deal with the machine, and it's much better, because you get to the know the machine. I had some bad experience when I was not in self-care. When I was beginning I did not know the machines, so if something was wrong, I was always afraid, and now I know the machine, it's much better, because now I can deal with it right away if I need to. I am used to it now, it's been almost eight years, a lot of time, I can do it easily, no problem.

I meet a lot of new people on dialysis. It is like some kind of insurance, sometimes you ask the other people if they feel okay, and they say, "Yeah I feel all right", so you say if he feels all right, I can feel all right too.

I do almost the same things I was doing before, the only thing is, let's say I go to a party, I have to control myself, I can't drink what I want, or the amount I want, even if I can eat some of the things, on others I have to pass. You have to have self-control to do that, because if you don't, you're going to be in trouble.

In a way I think that if you keep busy, doing something, even working a few hours a day or a few days a week, it's better for your health.

Now I work in a bar for a few days. I'm busy, I talk with a lot of people. These people, a lot of them don't know even my problem and it's better for me. I found that at the beginning, if I put in the application for a job I have that problem, right away I will be refused. The better thing is to not say what I have. I lived like that for many years. I had one interesting job, I worked there for so many years, it was one of the biggest furniture stores in Montreal. It was a big company and I worked there for eight years. I never told them that I had a transplant, so I think it was a better way to do it. I am still discriminated against. Where I work now, if I say to them that I am on dialysis, they don't want me to work for them. They will say, "He's a sick guy, he can't do the job like the other people." It's the way they think.

32

Maurice Kouri, a 72-year-old man, began hemodialysis nine months ago.

Last Christmas I was rushed to the hospital because my kidneys had totally failed. Prior to that incident, the doctors had been asking me for several months to get ready for dialysis but I always asked them to put it off. Finally that incident happened and there was no other choice for me but to start dialysis. Thank God, I feel a 100 percent better since I started my treatment and I have not regretted my decision since. The doctors have put my name on the list for a kidney transplant and I hope that someday my turn will come.

Hemodialysis improved my condition for sure. Before hemodialysis I could hardly walk because I used to feel very tired. But now I can walk using a cane. I used to hate the needles in my arm but it did not take long before I got used to them. I have no trouble with the diet limitations. The only inconvenience I find about dialysis is the four-hour wait in the clinic.

Once I am at home I sleep around 10 at night and I get up the following morning around six. I have a small business and I call up a few customers and that makes the time go by quickly. The business keeps my mind busy and that way I think less of hemodialysis.

The ironic thing about dialysis is that it made me see my children more than I used to do before. My children take their turn to come with me to the hospital and this way I am constantly in touch with my family. I have cared about my kids throughout my life so I guess it's their turn to take care of their dad. My grandchildren are also one of the reasons I want to stick around to be able to see them grow. The nurses are very lovely and are so good to me. I read the Bible a little bit and I thank God for my being around everyday. That may be one of the reasons why I am coming along fine.

I advise those who were diagnosed with kidney failure not to hesitate when the doctor advises them to take dialysis and to go right ahead. They'll definitely feel the difference after they start on it. I am gonna stick with it the whole way and if I have a chance for a transplant I may go for it.

33

A 68-year-old man who wishes to remain anonymous began hemodialysis two months ago.

I was working in an executive position. Doctors told me that if I wanted to live, I had to get away from the stress. I left my job in 1990 when I got sick. Two months ago I came to the hospital for pneumonia and I had a cardiac arrest. From thereon, I started dialysis. I don't really know if the kidney collapsed because I'm still waiting for the results of the tests. In August 1990, I made a choice between CAPD and hemodialysis and chose the latter. At that time, the doctor introduced a fistula into my arm. The reason for the removal of my left kidney was that it was covered by a tumor. Now I have one kidney left which is functioning at a very low level.

Coping with dialysis depends essentially on how the patient takes it. I had to accept it. I had no choice. Morally, I feel that I have lost my freedom. I am tied to dialysis machines. One has the choice to either face life or death. When I am not on dialysis, I enjoy my time with the family. I have a wife, two daughters and grandchildren.

I can't play sports anymore. I stopped playing tennis two years ago and I stopped swimming. I continue to walk but I can't walk in cold weather. Patients going on dialysis shouldn't be scared, but they should have knowledge of the various types of dialysis before making their choice of which type is more convenient. The schedules for dialysis are provided according to availability and not according to the demand of the individual. This creates problems.

In 1990, I had to change my eating habits in terms of volume and type of food in order to safeguard the one asset left which was the kidney functioning at 20 percent. It is difficult. You have to eliminate many vegetables, fruits, juice and salt. The doctors have helped me for the last six years and are still helping and guiding me.

34

Theophanis Mantzikas, a 58-year-old man, began hemodialysis a year and a half ago.

I started dialysis on April 23rd 1995. In 1991, I had an accident at work and got a hernia. After the operation I had a big problem. I had another operation in 1996 to fix this problem. But after the second operation I still had pain. I live with a lot of pain and I'm very depressed because of it. I saw many doctors and I saw the pain group and they told me that I would live with the pain for the rest of my life. Because of the pain I have high blood pressure. I had several examinations and started to have problems with my heart and kidney. I cried everyday. I was working at the same job for 20 years. I had a very big problem with my boss because I couldn't work very well and there were fights everyday. The doctor in nephrology told me that my kidney wasn't good and after one month I went for dialysis. My wife doesn't want me to have another operation because I may not be able to walk afterwards. I can't have sex because I have too much pain. The doctor said that if I have a kidney transplant they will remove a hernia that is now in my stomach. I asked for a kidney transplant and the doctors told me that it will take maybe two months to one year. It has already been seven months. I can't work now because nobody will hire me because I have to come to the hospital for dialysis. As well, I can't work with a hernia. I take a few steps and I'm out of breath. Before dialysis my whole body was very itchy but after I started dialysis the itching stopped.

My life is good. My family is good. All my children went to school. There was never a problem. One child is an accountant, another is a telephone technician and another is a teacher. My wife is very good... no problem. We never fight but she doesn't want me to have another operation because she knows that all night my hand is on my side and all night I have pain. I was taking a very strong medication for the hernia and the doctors told me not to take it for more than three years. My stomach has opened inside five times because of  too many prescription drugs for the hernia. I believe that if I don't come for dialysis I will die but with the hernia I won't die. But the hernia causes me pain, not the kidney. I have pain daytime and nighttime.

My daughter is married in Greece and she has one girl and one boy. My son is married here and he has twin boys who are four months old. I go there and I play with the children and they come to my house. When I see the children I'm happy and I forget everything. I forget all my problems. I would tell new patients to come for dialysis because it's good because it cleans the blood and if it weren't for the machines everybody would die. I don't eat bananas or oranges. They are high in potassium. I take care of myself.

If I get a transplant I would like to start work but I don't know if I can because of the hernia. My friend had a kidney transplant three and a half months ago. He lives across from my house and he's very happy and I'm happy for him too. I see that his life has changed. His kidney is working very well. I'm going to have this operation one day too.

35

A 47-year-old man who wishes to remain anonymous began treatment 16 years ago. His treatments have included hemodialysis and a kidney transplant.

I was working in Saudi Arabia and one morning I was feeling sick, I didn't have much energy and I was vomiting. I was working with an exploration team looking for oil and we lived all together in a type of compound. I used to do Taé kwan do and all that stuff and suddenly I couldn't keep up with the other people. So I saw the cook from our compound and he asked me what was wrong and I said that I didn't know, you know, I feel like vomiting. He then said, "Do you drink"? And I told him, not particularly, no. He thought maybe it could be my liver. One morning I woke up and my face was yellow and I realized something was really wrong so I went to the hospital and they did some blood tests and found that my kidneys were gone. So I asked the doctor what that meant and he said "Don't worry". But, what about my job? He said "Don't worry, you don't have to worry, you just have a small machine and you just put it on your belt". He didn't know! He was a doctor but he didn't know anything. I saw this machine and I didn't think it would fit on my belt. I couldn't come directly back here because I was too sick already so I had to go across to England with my ex-wife. But because I was a foreigner in England, they wouldn't dialyze me and yet I was still too sick to get all the way back to Canada. So the only hope was for me to go to Italy. So I went to Italy and they accepted me right away to do it, they are much nicer people. It took a while to recuperate but I was starting to feel much better and my blood was getting cleaned and so I could travel back to Montréal.

I didn't cope at all, no way, you don't cope. You think people are courageous or something, but no, there is just no other way. I have a daughter and I do it for her. So now I take care of my daughter. I tutor her in school and I do everything for her. I am not happy with my situation but it is not a matter of being happy, you have a situation and you have to deal with it. You realize that you have this situation and you have two paths and you choose the one you want. Either you let yourself die or you continue on. This is just a small walk for us, the end is not on this earth. You have to go through these problems and we say that God will call you and it is different for different people. Some people lose their families, some lose their money, so maybe through this he wants me to do something else. For example, before this I was always travelling and I would hardly see my daughter, so from this we have a closer bond, this is something good that has happened.

It took some time because people don't explain to you exactly what is happening to you. But then it brings you closer to things you were away from before, like God and other things and suddenly life seems more simple. I am smiling a lot more now, people always ask me why I am so happy. I am just happy. Before I didn't understand the situation, I didn't understand the purpose and meaning because I got sick when I was 30. Thirty is just the beginning of your life, you don't understand so many things. You start understanding things when you are 40. It took a long time but now I understand. You think that you are the healthiest person in the world and that you'll never get sick. But it is just waiting for you around the corner and you have to expect it. People don't expect it, I didn't.

For people starting dialysis I can tell them just from my experiences that there is trouble ahead. People leave you. I think because they are scared maybe that it is contagious or something like that. People are so ignorant about a lot of things, not just this. Friends also just disappear because you are not fun any more. They want you to go out, they want to drink, they want to eat, and you just sit in front of them and say, "I can't drink, I can't eat". Okay so I do that now and then but they just stay away and say why bother with him?

New people they come here to see the place and they bring them to talk to me for a couple of minutes. I tell them, "Don't worry", but they know the truth and they cry. "What am I going to do with my job and my life? I won't have a baby?" And they start crying. So you tell them "No, it is not like this, it will be okay". But it's the truth, when you get sick it is bad. But you have to try to understand the meaning of the thing because as I said, if you see the whole picture, you are not alone, meaning that it happens to everybody. I mean this is the way things are, some people they cross the street and they get hit and they die. So it is not a big deal. We are all afraid of death.

So you see people have to live their own experiences. You can write a thousand books, but different things happen to everybody and sometimes it is not a sickness but it is something else that is worse. So you see, people have to accept it. We have to be like a piece of bamboo. You see with bamboo, when there is a strong wind it just bends a little because of the wind but it doesn't break. It doesn't try to resist. That is what we should do. If some problems occur we just go down and go with whatever happens because we have no other choice. If you want to resist, you break and that is it.

36

David Nelson, a 51-year-old man, began treatment five years ago. His treatments have included peritoneal dialysis and a kidney transplant.

I found out that I had kidney disease when my daughter was four years old. That's when she was diagnosed with polycystic kidney disease, and I was told that in order for her to have this disease, one of the parents must also have it. So my wife and I got tested, and it turned out that I was the one who had it. That happened 26 years ago, I was 25 years old when I found out.

The next major development occurred five years ago. One day, I was playing softball, and I had a little accident while sliding in to first base. When I went to the hospital, they observed the state of my kidneys, and decided that it was time for me to start dialysis. I chose peritoneal dialysis, and I continued this for three years. During this time, my wife gave me unbelievable support. She and my daughter were incredibly supportive, as were the children my wife had from a previous marriage. My doctor also provided me with a lot of support, since he treated not only my body but also my mind. As well, my work also gave me all kinds of support at the time. I had a private office, so I was able to do my treatments in the office when I had to. But, to be quite honest, back then I did not think that I needed support. It was only after the fact that I realized how these people had really been supporting me all along, and how important their support had been.

I found that being on dialysis really put a time restriction on things. It limited the places to which I could go, because I always had to have a certain amount of time set aside for my treatment. This affected some of my activities, such as playing golf. Gradually the kidney problem led me to become more irritable, and I began to snap at people more easily. Around that time, I also noticed that I was slowing down, and that my condition was deteriorating. I did not think that anything was physically wrong with me, I just thought that I was getting old. But then I got a kidney transplant, and I realized that I was not getting old at all.

If anyone were to ask me whether I would recommend getting a kidney transplant, the answer would definitely be yes. My kidney transplant made my life a lot better than it was before. Since I got the transplant, I find myself much easier to get along with. Before, I used to use my exchanges as an excuse when I wanted to leave a conversation. Now, I find that I enjoy being with people and talking to them.

Recently, I have also started volunteering in a hemodialysis unit. I was talked into this by my doctor, who thought it would do me a world of good. And he was right! I started doing it a few months ago, and I think that it has helped me in several ways. I'm a very shy person, and usually I don't go out of my way to meet anyone. Once I know somebody, then I feel comfortable talking to that person. But now that I started volunteering, I tend to make a little extra effort to meet people. I'm still shy sometimes, but volunteering has helped quite a bit. I think that I have also been helpful to some of the patients. When I come by, some of them are glad to see me and talk to me quite a bit. Then again, some of them fall asleep when I'm around, so who knows?

Since I got my transplant, my health has also been unbelievable. In fact, I hardly ever get headaches anymore. I can also do many more things than I was able to while on dialysis. Back then, when I used to play golf, I had to use an electric cart because I could never walk around 18 holes. Now I don't use the cart anymore, because I can actually walk around the 18 holes.

I think that in this situation the true heroes are not the dialysis and transplant patients, but the people who donate the kidneys, their families, and the doctors who put the kidneys in and make them work. Without them, there would be no such thing as a kidney transplant. It takes courage to do something like that, and it takes people who are willing to do it for others. As for me, my part was easy. I just had to sit back and let it happen.

37

Mr. Georges Zeitouni, a 77-year-old man, began hemodialysis four years ago.

I started dialysis following a heart bypass operation. I had my first dialysis treatment just before the operation to allow the cardiac surgeon to reach my heart more easily. At the time, I was very swollen because my body was retaining a lot of water, and due to that I had my first dialysis treatment, and afterwards I simply continued the dialysis.

Before I started coming to the dialysis centre I had lots of activities, but now that I have to come to the hospital on a regular basis, I don't have as much time as before. This surely made for a lot of changes in my normal activities. I was forced to ask for retirement because I obviously couldn't continue my work at the same pace. Given my age, it was also time to take my retirement. I was a lawyer and it's a very interesting profession, especially if you like it, as I did. In any case, it's true that when you reach a certain age and need dialysis as well, it is necessary to stop working.

Dialysis has changed some things for me in the sense that now, the most interesting thing in my life is coming to the hospital for my treatments. It hasn't changed my relationship with people, other than now I am less available. Otherwise, it doesn't change anything else, because dialysis is not something that shows. Away from the hospital and from the machine one is like a normal person and no one knows you are on dialysis. Now that I have retired, the only difference is that instead of going to work, I go to the hospital for my dialysis treatments.

To new patients I say, you must be courageous, because after all is said and done, dialysis works well. I would say to these patients that they mustn't be impatient, but more than that, they must be very patient. This isn't just a play on words, it's something very important to accept. I think that you mustn't get nervous, that you must accept dialysis in a "cool" way in the slang sense of the word. Believe that everything is easy and it will just become routine. It is extremely important to always plan your activities and travels according to the demands of the dialysis treatments.

I don't think I'm very brave, but rather I think that dialysis is a necessity for my health and for my life. At times I feel nostalgic for my profession, but given my age I accept the fact that I cannot work on a regular basis. To all new patients my message is simply, "Good luck, you'll get used to it, and that's life".

38

Johanne, a 59 year-old-woman, began hemodialysis one month ago.

I have had diabetes for 16 years which caused my kidneys to fail. Just this last spring I had to pass all kinds of tests that confirmed that I did have a bigger problem than I realized. It was only in November when the doctor decided that I should go on dialysis. I can't do home dialysis because of my vision and I also had a tumor removed from my ovary in 1980, the same time that they discovered I was diabetic. I also get hypoglycemic reactions, so I wouldn't be able to cope with peritoneal dialysis.

My husband and two children keep their feelings to themselves with regard to me going through dialysis. I guess they all expected it and they each cope with it in their way. Every Saturday night I have a heavy date with a machine! I'm tired after a session on dialysis but I'll get over it, I guess.

I come for the treatment so I guess I have accepted it to a point. I was never angry that I had to go on dialysis. I figured that when the time would come it would come. I still do everything that I want to do but my life has changed because it's dependent upon a machine. It's not easy. The nurses don't like to make it sound as if it's bad but rather that it's a "normal" situation. It really isn't. It could go bad and yet it could go smoothly. Once you're on dialysis, you can get many different symptoms until they figure out how your particular system works. They didn't prepare me for what I would be experiencing. I wasn't prepared for symptoms such as headaches, blurry vision, nausea, and at times diarrhea. I feel very degraded that a machine can cause me to have diarrhea. I think that being on dialysis for four hours is just a little bit too long. When you're needled and it doesn't go right, it's pain you don't expect. This is what I was not prepared for. I wasn't informed well enough. I guess the doctors and nurses know what could happen but they don't discuss the unpleasant reactions. I'm the type that likes to know what to expect. I'm learning the hard way through experience.

Each session on dialysis is a new experience because I don't know how it's going to work out and I'm always afraid of the unknown. I think that not knowing is the worst problem. There is nobody that really wants to talk about what they went through on dialysis. My mother had dialysis and she wouldn't talk about it except to say that she hated it. Even though my mother was on dialysis and I used to come and visit her, I really didn't know what was going on. It's only through experience that you really know.

39

A 70-year-old man who wishes to remain anonymous began hemodialysis 10 years ago.

When I was 12 years old, I started working in the lumber camps. I worked in the bush, cutting trees. Then, the Second World War started, so I enlisted and served for six and a half years. However, in 1941 I was taken prisoner in China on Christmas day. The British had no planes or ships to support us at the time, and so I remained prisoner in and around Hong Kong for three years. When I was released, I returned to Canada only to discover that I had tuberculosis in my kidney and bladder. The doctors told me that I would have to remain in the hospital for one year. I ended up staying in the hospital for six and a half years.

During those years, I spent my time in a hospital for tuberculosis patients and in a veterans' hospital. I also worked part-time on a farm for a farmer that I knew. I remember that before I found out about the tuberculosis I had a sweetheart, and I had been looking forward to seeing her. When I found out about it, I realized that I would not be able to see her for a long time because tuberculosis patients had to be quarantined. So I told her to go marry someone else, and that was that. After those years in the hospital, I was released and had to come to the hospital for check-ups once a month. However, in 1949 I had to have one kidney removed, and in 1968 only half of my remaining kidney was functioning. Finally, in 1986 my kidney function was reduced to the point where I had to begin dialysis.

Of course, I didn't like the idea of starting dialysis at the beginning, but with the way I was feeling I would have taken any treatment. In the end, it worked out pretty well. I'm still here even after 10 years of dialysis, although I have my on-and-off days. Many times, I wanted to quit dialysis and I almost did. I wanted to go up north into the bush, surround myself with a big pile of trees, make a big fire and cremate myself. Just last year, I told the doctors that I was thinking of quitting.

I have to say that I have improved since then. One thing that keeps me going is all the nice people who are in the dialysis unit. I come here and I talk to the nurses and doctors. I joke around with them all the time. This is the only place where I feel alive. The doctors here are all very good to me, and I like all of them. Also, there is one doctor here who is especially good to me. I have decided that if I ever win the lottery, I will send it all to her.

Actually, I don't really mind coming to dialysis. I like it, and I prefer it to staying home and watching television or staring at four walls. This is especially true in the winter. As for support, I am not too religious, and I don't have much family living nearby. The only family member who lives close to me is my sister. Yet every summer, my family comes to see me, and many nephews and nieces come for a visit. But personally, I like the outdoors, and I don't like having too many people around. I liked living in the bush, where I could hunt, fish some trout and eat that for lunch. Now I can't do that anymore, because I cannot get around too well. But those were the days...

I think that compared to being a prisoner in Hong Kong, coming to dialysis doesn't seem so bad, and I appreciate it. When I was a prisoner, it was only work, work, work and no rest. Also, we often had only rice to eat, and that was difficult at first. Sometimes we received some Chinese cabbage or fish. Due to that, now I never complain about food. But during my life, I have already had 16 operations and now I am at the point where I have had enough. If I need another operation to save my life, I don't want it. I think that I have had my share of illness. Sometimes I get sick at home, and I become discouraged. So I have signed a D.N.R (Do Not Resuscitate) form here at the hospital, to specify that I don't want any special resuscitation procedures performed if something should happen to me. I have also had my cremation paid for in advance. I don't like big funerals, and I think that they cost too much money. As long as I feel no pain, I am all right.

40

Wilford Smith, a 66-year-old man, began treatment 27 years ago.
His treatments have consisted of hemodialysis and a kidney transplant.

This is my second time on dialysis. I was diagnosed with renal failure in 1970 and I started out on dialysis. I got a transplant in 1975, on April 28th, I remember that. With the transplant I had a little bout of diabetes that was brought on by the steroid drugs that you have to take for the antirejection. I had many bouts of infections at one time or another and in 1981 I ended up with them having to remove one of the native kidneys. It was defective. Since then I was relatively free of infections and things like that but in 1993 they felt that the new kidney was giving up so I had

to come back onto dialysis again until I got another one. It is just me and my wife. My two sons have grown up and moved out so it is just she and I left. She gave me the encouragement and what not as much as she could because she didn't know too much about it at the time. One of the first doctors that I met here I've known now for more than 20 years and the other one I've known for quite a while and then there are a lot of nurses here that I know from the old hospital so they have all really been here for me. Doctor "X" has been especially helpful, he is the one that I have known the longest and he is very good.

The time spent on dialysis is not too bad. I have four days off and sometimes I have to shift appointments and meetings around but you learn to live with it. It's really no problem. I'm here at six in the morning. I live out of town and it takes a while to get here but I'm an early bird so I don't mind. I'm usually the first one on so I'm usually the first one off. It still leaves me half a day. I'm here on Saturday so Sunday and Monday are more like my weekends and if I am going to travel, it will be then. It hasn't cut down my travelling too much except that it is a little more inconvenient. I've been down to Barbados a few times since I have been on dialysis. I happened to pick an island that has the only dialysis unit in the Caribbean other than Jamaica. The first year that I was on dialysis I had to be in Toronto and they took me at their hospital. They have a reciprocal agreement with this hospital and others in the area sort of like we'll take your patient if you'll take ours. I have also been down to Halifax. Barbados, what could be better than a dialysis unit where the birds are flying around the building.

When you have the transplant it is obviously very good because you can go away when you want and you don't have to worry too much about it. You just have to schedule your time at the clinic. Towards the end I only had to go about once every three months so that was good because if I was going to go away I would just ask to be scheduled a week earlier or a week later and they would do that. After you have the transplant, your immunity goes down so I had some little problems but that was about 20 years ago and we've taken care of most of those problems now.

No, I don't consider myself a hero. I'm doing what I have to, that's all there is to it. I am doing this because I don't like the alternative. I don't consider anybody that is on this any kind of a hero, they are just coping. As a matter of fact, I'd like to see the word hero changed because I don't think that's a good definition of it. To be a hero is if I happen to run into the street to save someone who is about to get smacked by a car or something like that but that is heroism a bit, this is not heroism. This is putting up with what you have to put up with.

I try to run my life as normally as possible. Dialysis is part of my life, it doesn't run me. I joined up with the Boy Scouts years ago because my wife was chairman of our local group and now she is president of our district. I'm the treasurer on the district council now as well and they keep on electing me back so I must be doing something right. If I don't feel up to going to a meeting I just don't go. I'll go the month after. I am also chairman of the banquet committee so I look after all that.

All I can say is to cope with the situation and put your name on the waiting list and sooner or later a kidney will become available and then you can get back to a more or less normal life. It can't be completely normal because you still have to come in occasionally for blood tests and there might be some side effects from the medication but all you can do is cope the best you can.

41

Pauline Nethersole, a 73-year-old woman, began hemodialysis five years ago.

I found out that I had to begin dialysis when I fainted three mornings in a row. On the third morning, I was in the washroom and my daughter heard a thump. She came in and told me that I had to go to the hospital because maybe there was something wrong. Personally, I thought that I probably had the flu. Then, when I was in the hospital and lying on my hospital bed, the doctor came in and told me that I had a kidney problem. I said, "No!" and my doctor said, "Yes!".

When I had my first tests of kidney function, I was brought on a visit to the dialysis unit and I saw everything. Then, before I had to start dialysis, the doctors wanted me to come for another visit, but I refused to go see the machines. I couldn't look at all those people lying there attached to the machines. I don't know, I guess I was a bit upset. I thought that if my doctor had been more alert, maybe I wouldn't have had to go on dialysis. However, at that point, there was not much I could do about it. I had hung on as long as I could, refusing to start dialysis until the last possible minute. Eventually, I realized that I just had to start dialysis, because I was sick and I couldn't move. My doctor was also insisting that I begin the treatment. I realized that there was no point complaining about it, because I just had to do it and I could not change that.

I have a very strong will, and I am not going to let this knock me down. However, I have to say that it has affected what I can do and where I can go. A few years ago, I used to go down to Florida, but now I am afraid of going and getting sick down there. So I have not been there in a couple of years. In general, I love to travel, and I also used to go to Toronto all the time. Now, I have to make sure I can get my dialysis treatment there before I go. In any case, I don't find that I have the strength to run around anymore.

I think that I have to take dialysis with a smile, and I do not want to let it get me down. I guess this energy and optimism is just something I was born with. There are also things which are helpful, such as going out. That allows me to forget about everything and make a change. Going away somewhere is also a change from the regular routine of my house, but unfortunately I do not travel often anymore. Now, there are only two of us in the house, myself and my husband. My children are not around anymore, they're all grown and gone. My husband doesn't want a pet, so sometimes it gets lonesome, just the two of us. We both get along day by day. Sometimes I play solitaire or do crossword puzzles, and that brightens up my time.

I like life, and I figure that if I want to live, I have to keep going. Sometimes, when I get really sick, it gets me down, so I shut out the bad feelings. I have a grandson, so I think of him and how much I want to see him finish university. Every time I feel sick, he tells me, "You can't die now, Grandma, you have your grandson". I have three other grand-children too, but he is the only boy. In general, my family was very supportive of me when I started dialysis. They were always telling me what I should do or should not do. I wish they would not do that! They also always tell me not to cheat on my diet, but you have to cheat sometimes.

The first day that I went to dialysis, I could not wait to get out of there, and I ran out of the room when I was finished. I can't believe I actually ran! Now, I don't run anymore, but I just walk out slowly. Dialysis is just like anything else, in that I became accustomed to it. I have accepted it, although sometimes I wonder, "Why me?". But I know that everyone has some sort of problem, and I guess this is not the worst thing that could have happened to me.

42

Mario King, a 66-year-old man, began hemodialysis five years ago.

My kidney troubles started in 1991 and were caused by diabetes. I had the choice between peritoneal dialysis and hemodialysis, and I picked the latter because there were less chances of infection. Also I did not choose peritoneal dialysis because I'd have to do it at home, and there would be no one to watch me. Right now I am having some blood tests done in preparation for a kidney transplant. To this point I refused to have a kidney transplant because I am taking the hemodialysis well. Hemodialysis does not really interfere with my life except for having to spend three days a week in the hemodialysis clinic. But lately I have been pressured by the doctors to consider the transplant because they told me that I was going to have breakdowns in my health system if I stayed too long on hemodialysis. And somewhere along the line I will have to say yes or no and take it from there. Every once in a while people who had kidney transplants come to the hemodialysis clinic and they tell us how remarkably well they feel. I have not met anyone who said that they would not do it again. However, I have seen only the people whose kidney transplant has succeeded. I would like to talk to a few people whose transplant did not go so well and see what they say about kidney transplant.

When I found out that I had to go on hemodialysis, I was devastated. I could not believe it was happening to me. From the age of 18 to 30, I was a professional athlete and I was never sick a day in my life. I played football, I boxed, and I wrestled. I could not believe it was going to come to that, and I was scared to death of every medical intervention. I did not want any support from anybody. I was sort of hiding; I did not talk to my friends about my condition because I was telling myself that my kidney ailment would soon go away. Now I realize that the more you talk about something, the less serious it seems to be. In the end, I got so sick from the toxins in my body, that I asked the doctors to put me on dialysis. I am a lot better now than I used to be. You get things done to you and you feel some improvement in your health. Then you realize that those medical interventions were not so bad after all. For instance, I just had an arterial surgery on my leg this past February and it turned out to be very successful. Initially I thought I was going to die because that was my first real surgery, except for the time when they operated on my arm to place the fistula. I had a lot of hard time accepting it in the beginning because ignorance is fear. So the more you find out about a medical procedure the less you will be bothered and scared to death from it.

Before I started dialysis, I used to feel very sick. Now, I don't consider myself sick anymore and I am following everything that I am supposed to do very closely and I live fairly well. I used to go to the gym and helped the kids but I could not keep it up because it was too tiring. I still go to the gym a couple of days a week just to see the guys and hang around but I can't take on any programs because I don't know how I will feel the next day. One of the problems that I have right now is that I don't have any appetite at all. I have to eat several times a day because I am diabetic. If it was not for that I would not eat. So the limitations that dialysis imposes on its patients do not affect me at all because there is nothing that I would like to have that I can't have. The restraints on the liquid intake is pretty tough, because being a diabetic, I feel always thirsty. So that's a tough one to control.

The biggest difference in coping with kidney disease and dialysis was having to come here three days a week. I was working when I fell sick and the doctor stopped me from working. So I went on a disability pension until the age of 65, and now I am on the old age pension. The biggest difference in my life is not earning money. My pension set up is not so bad but it is not like working. I don't find that I have too much time on my hands. I wonder sometimes where the time goes.

I have a girlfriend and a sister. I don't discuss my situation with my sister because I don't see her that often. We're close but we don't get into each other's lives. My girlfriend has been very supportive. I met her the same week I got sick and we live together now.

I would suggest to anybody who is preparing for dialysis to find out anything they can about it and not to hide from it because their kidney problem is there with them and it is not going anywhere. There is so much to dialysis and it is more frightening looking at it than being on it. If I had found out more about the dialysis machine I would not have been as apprehensive as I was. It is very important to keep the spirits up, and the morale high. You should feel fortunate because you can always see people in worse shape than you are. People with amputated legs and people with terminal diseases are definitely worse off than you. What I did was very wrong when I tried to hide from the truth and I was fortunate enough to finally face up to it. You just have to grab it by the throat and go after it. Your condition will not go away so you better get on with it and do the best you can.

43

Robert Drury, a 73-year-old man, began hemodialysis a year and a half ago.

My health problems started in 1970 when the doctors found out that I had high blood pressure. I guess the fact of having high blood pressure also affected my kidneys to a point where my kidneys have failed. On June 29, 1995, my doctor suggested that I start the dialysis treatment and to date I have had 221 of these treatments and I never missed one of my appointments. I drive to the hospital about 25 kilometers each way and I have always been able to report here on time. I might also mention that I am part of a study in Winnipeg for ex-pilots during the war and the study is still going on. I forward information once a year about my condition and the study has to do with 4,000 pilots, and the latest count was down to 2,500 pilots.

Prior to starting dialysis, I attended several meetings in the Royal Victoria Hospital about dialysis, during a period of two months, and the staff briefed us on what to expect from dialysis. Of course my wife attended the meetings as well as me, so she was prepared for it and so was I. The staff also made us visit the dialysis rooms a couple of times and I saw the patients lined up and that did not bother me. I did not object to having dialysis because my doctor knows what is best for me and I listen to him because he's the boss. It's always important for me to follow my diet as recommended by the dietitian.

My life is almost the same as before I started on dialysis. Today I drive my car to the hospital without any problems at all. I feel fortunate because a lot of people I know who are on dialysis depend on somebody else to take them to and away from the hospital. Being able to drive my car gives me independence and freedom.

I got the greatest support from the nurses and the doctors at the dialysis clinic. I also receive a lot of support from my family and I see my wonderful grandchildren pretty regularly. They come to have supper with me every second Sunday night.

Before you get on dialysis, you should watch your blood pressure and avoid doing all the things that will put you on dialysis. I guess all my life I enjoyed going out and drinking. Maybe I should have cut back on that years ago but who knows. If you want to live, you've got to take your treatment. I am resigned now that I'll be doing this for the rest of my life. As long as I am able to drive, I'll be fine. It will be foolish of you not to go on dialysis if that's the only option you have. I figured if I follow the doctor's orders and the diet as closely as possible, I should have a few more years of life around to enjoy the grandchildren and to keep driving my car.

44

Martha Zanna, a 42-year-old woman, began treatment 30 years ago. Her treatments have been hemodialysis, peritoneal dialysis and three kidney transplants.

I was 10 years old when I found out that something was wrong with my kidneys. Finally, I had a test done and it showed that I had polycystic kidneys. I had to start receiving many blood transfusions, and when I was 10 years old, I started peritoneal dialysis. At 13, I had my first kidney transplant. I was scared at the time, but my mother told me that I was always a very courageous child.

The first time I had my dialysis treatment, I was very scared because I got sick and I had convulsions. I saw all these tubes coming in and out of me, but no one had explained to me what they were for. I also had to stay in the hospital overnight for the first time, and I recall seeing many kids in the ward. They were all sleeping, but I stayed awake looking at them. I had no idea why I was there. Luckily, there was a nice nurse there who encouraged me and gave me reassurance. There was also a small daycare center in the hospital where the kids could play. Going to that daycare had a strong impact on me, and to this day, if I hear certain songs, they remind me of that time. That was my first experience in the hospital, but afterwards I got used to it. The next time I went, it did not bother me.

About four months after I changed to hemodialysis, I got a call for a kidney transplant. This happened very unexpectedly, because everyone thought that I would have to wait a long time. But there was a good match, and everything got done very quickly. At nine o'clock at night, we got the call, and less than two hours later I was in the hospital. I was very scared that time, and I was crying and screaming all night. This happened in 1968, and it was in the papers because the donor had also donated a heart to someone, and it was the first time a heart transplant had been done here. So, the donor had donated a heart and two kidneys to people, and I had received one of the kidneys. Later, I found out that the person who received the heart transplant eventually died, as did the lady who received the second kidney. I was the only one who remained alive. But when I woke up from the operation, the only thing I wanted to do was go home.

Unfortunately, things were not that simple. I had problems after the operation, and I had to stay in the hospital for 40 days. Then, I went home, but only three days later, I developed a high fever and I had to return to the hospital. I cried a lot, because I didn't want to go back there. But I had no choice, and while I was there my kidney stopped functioning. I had another operation so the doctors could see what was wrong. They found that blood had clotted in one of the veins related to my kidney. Due to all this, I had to spend a year in the hospital, with a tube coming out of my kidney to help it along. I lost a lot of weight, and became really skinny. But with time, I gradually got better, and my kidney started to work properly once again. I gained weight, got back my energy, and did not have any more problems with the kidney for 21 years.

During those years, I led a good life. Then, insidiously, my creatinine began rising. This meant that my transplanted kidney wasn't working like it should anymore. Soon after, I had to begin dialysis again. At first, I didn't want to hear anything about dialysis, because I didn't believe I would really need it. I didn't realize I would actually have to start over again after all those years. However, this time I had my dialysis with bicarbonate, and that eliminated all the bad reactions and sickness which dialysis had caused me to have in the past. After a year, I became used to dialysis again.

Two years later, my cousin decided that she wanted to give me one of her kidneys. I absolutely refused, but she insisted so much that I eventually accepted and had my second kidney transplant. It worked beautifully for a year, but then I went on a tour of Italy for the summer and I started to get sick. I did not want to believe that I was rejecting. I knew what it was like to live without dialysis. The doctors tried as hard as they could to save my kidney, but it didn't work.

Then, seven months ago I received a third kidney transplant. Now I am happy, because I've had a miracle. I live a completely normal life now. I work in a daycare center with kids, and I go out to relax when I can. My parents are always beside me, and that helps me a lot. In the past, their constant presence gave me a lot of courage. The love of my parents has really helped me through a lot. That is how my parents have always been with their children. My sister also had the same disease that I have, and my mom gave her one of her kidneys. Unfortunately, it didn't work, and my sister passed away.

My parents say that I have a strong character, but I think that everyone would do the same things I did in order to stay alive. I wanted to live, and I did what I had to do. My experiences have made me stronger, and now I appreciate life more. Even while I was on dialysis, I still went to work at the daycare, and I still went out to party afterwards. I just wanted to live and do everything. I think that what is important is how a person looks at life. If someone wants to live, it is important to make the best of their situation. It's all in the hands of destiny, but God's help has encouraged me. I think that to be happy in the next world, it is important to take the good with the bad in this world. Life is not a bed of roses, but it is important to have faith.

45

An 81-year-old woman who wishes to remain anonymous began treatment three and a half years ago. Her treatment has consisted of hemodialysis and peritoneal dialysis.

Approximately 10 to 15 years ago, during a regular check-up, my primary doctor told me that he had found some crystals in my urine sample but he told me not to worry because everything was all right. I spoke to my friend about the doctor's finding and he urged me to go see a nephrologist because the crystals in my urine were not normal. The nephrologist sent me for an ultrasound and discovered that I had a cyst in my kidney. My kidneys gradually failed and there came a time when they finally collapsed. I had the choice between the peritoneal and the hemodialysis. I chose the peritoneal dialysis because I wanted to avoid coming to the hospital three times a week for four hours. I stayed on the peritoneal dialysis for one year but then I had an infection. It took weeks before my infection healed. In the meantime I had a catheter placed in my neck and I continued my dialysis. Later on I had a fistula placed in my arm and that's when I started on hemodialysis.

When I found out that I had to be on dialysis I was very depressed. Sometimes I felt so bad that I wished I were dead. The hospital assigned a social worker to my case and I told her that I was crying because I saw dialysis as only an extension to my agony. My anxiety was amplified when I had the infection from the peritoneal dialysis. The catheter made things more complicated because I had to lay on my left side during the whole treatment. However, since I started on hemodialysis I feel much better. Sometimes I feel so perfect that I would not know I had kidney failure. The only inconvenience that I find in hemodialysis is when the nurse inserts the needle in my arm. But those needles do not bother me anymore.

I never went to anybody to discuss my situation; as a matter of fact I am still keeping it a secret until this day. I accepted kidney failure as part of my destiny. And having faith in God has helped me cope with my condition. I would have been much happier if my kidneys hadn't failed but what could I do? I had the condition already and I have to be thankful that dialysis existed.

Prior to being on dialysis I used to go skiing but when I was on peritoneal I did not dare to ski because I could fall down and hurt myself. I like to play ping-pong and I am still playing it but less than before I started on dialysis because I tend to get tired faster. But I blame that more on my age than on hemodialysis. I am still able to drive and that brings up my morale because I feel I am still independent.

If somebody is diagnosed with kidney failure, they should be very happy that hemodialysis exists because years ago when somebody had a kidney failure that was the end of their story. Try to forget about dialysis. It's very hard but it is not impossible. Follow your diet as closely as you can and your health will improve. Initially I saw dialysis as a sign of failure and as an extension of my agony, but later on I realized that it was my second chance to life.

46

Mario Zollo, a 56-year-old man, began hemodialysis one year ago.

I've been a diabetic since 1970, about 26 years, and I've never followed my diet but now I'm paying the price for it. I guess it's my diabetes that burned my kidneys and infected my foot. I had been working at the same place for 22 years but I stopped because of the problem with my foot, the diabetes and now my kidneys. Two years ago my driver's licence was taken away because my eyesight is not good. My sex drive is also finished because of my diabetes.

My wife went to be tested with me for a kidney transplant. Everything seems to be fine but I spoke to the doctor and he said that they're too busy, you know, for me to have a transplant, but I'm always waiting for a transplant. They said after the transplant, six months after, if everything is fine, they'll give me a pancreas transplant.

As for how I am going on with dialysis—I think it is very good because before I was always throwing up and I had headaches. I was really sick but since the year that I'm on dialysis, I'm feeling much better, much better—what a difference. I didn't know nothing about dialysis. I thought it would have hurt me or something, but thank God you know it didn't hurt at all. Only at the beginning a little when they try to adjust you but after, everything goes fine.

Thank God my wife is a strong woman. She gives me a lot of support on everything. There's nothing that makes me feel like a hero, but my wife and my son help give me the courage. It's not so bad so I don't really need help, but my wife she's always there, thank God for her. Transportation is sometimes a problem to get here and my son can sometimes help me on that when I'm stuck. I'm not crazy about coming here three times a week, but if it does you good, you know you have to.

About dialysis, I can't say too much about dialysis except don't be afraid, it's a good thing. I'll tell you—those headaches are gone and the vomiting too. I was going crazy, honest to God.

47

Jerry Yellen, a 59-year-old man, began treatment 14 years ago.
His treatments have been hemodialysis and two kidney transplants.

I had no idea about my kidney's failure until the time I came to the hospital, almost 20 years ago, to check some allergies that I had. The doctor took some blood and urine tests and found some proteins and some blood in my urine. Sometime later, I had a biopsy and the doctor found that 40 percent of my kidney was gone. I was watched by a doctor over several months, and slowly my kidneys deteriorated and I had to start dialysis in 1983. I was very fortunate because a little less than a year later, I received my first kidney transplant. Unfortunately, four years later I had to go back to hemodialysis because the transplanted kidney had failed. I stayed on hemodialysis until 1992 when I received my second transplant.

The idea of having dialysis did not set in my mind until the day I actually started on it. Even after they put the fistula in my arm I was still hoping that I wouldn't have to go on dialysis. I postponed it as long as I could but the doctor urged me to start on it and I finally did in 1983. Being on hemodialysis was not something that I wanted to go through my life doing. It was hard to accept the fact that I was going to be tied to a machine for the rest of my life and that I was going to be restricted on what I drank and what I ate but it was something I had to make friends with otherwise it would have given a lot of trouble.

My three children were very supportive and I was fortunate to have that. They used to come with me to the dialysis clinic and sit with me throughout the treatment and that was very good for my morale. My wife was very supportive. She stayed with me throughout my sickness. She followed the dietitian's rules when she cooked my meals. My friends were also supportive and tried to boost up my morale whenever I was depressed.

When I received my first transplant, I started taking different medications. Unfortunately the medications had some side effects. For instance my hip became infected and I had to have a hip replacement. The kidney transplant also affected my way of living and that was something I had to get used to all over again. Before I received the transplant I could not wait for my turn to come so that I can feel better. Unfortunately I found out that not everything becomes rosy and that I was not going to be one 100 percent like I initially thought.

However, once I had a transplant I didn't have to come to the hospital three times a week. My body stopped feeling itchy and I had a more regular heartbeat than when I was on dialysis. I had more energy and my blood pressure became steady. I did my exercise, walked and I tried to keep in shape. I ate with moderation because I realized that the antirejection drugs make people eat and that's how you start to gain weight and develop that moon face.

The transition from transplant to hemodialysis was very traumatic but I learned faster than I did the first time and I quickly accepted it. I had a lot of problems with my first transplant so I was sort of leery when the doctor told me that my turn had come for my second transplant. However I said to myself that I had to go for it and I am not sorry today.

I have my hobbies, I collect stamps and coins. I read the paper and I go out for walks. I talk to people and I don't think too much about my sickness. It's all in my positive attitude.

The best advice to anyone who is about to embark on any kind of kidney treatment is to find out all the information they can prior to starting on it. Once you know what will happen to you, it will be a lot easier to accept it because the unknown is very terrifying. You should feel lucky that there is a book like this where you have a preview of the coming attractions because when I started dialysis there was no information available and I had to learn about dialysis the hard way during my first year on it. You need to accept your problem and learn to live with it instead of fighting it because you will be fighting a losing battle. Everything takes time to heal and you need to be patient. You have to have hope because if you lose hope you will get nowhere.

48

This 40-year-old-man who is a hemodialysis patient wishes to remain anonymous.

POEM, TO MY DIALYSIS MACHINE

Dialysis, dialysis, hemo, hemo,
How do I love thee.
Allow me to concentrate the ways.
I love the way you ultrafiltrate me down
To a very respectable frown.
When my potassium is not okay
You respectfully show me the way.

Remove this, remove that,
Surely this is a langour that will pass.
Salt is an enemy of mine
Concentrating on pulling me down.
But you are strong, washing
All the grime from my prime.

I owe you so much
for your quiet disposition.
Now I understand why
I love and hate thee with ambition.

49

Alda McCaffrey, a 53-year-old woman, began treatment three years ago. She has undergone peritoneal dialysis and two kidney transplants.

When I was 17 I had to pass a medical to be admitted into Teachers' College at which time the doctor found some albumin in my urine and I had further testing done. I was informed that I had bad kidneys and that they may at some point cause me problems. I led a normal life and did everything that I wanted to do. In fact, I did a lot of equitation which could be a sport which jiggles your kidneys! I didn't have any problems that I know of, and every once in a while I would come to the hospital and I would have tests. I never really dwelled on the fact that I had this problem. About five years ago, I was informed that I should go on dialysis because my kidneys had failed. Previous to that I was getting swollen eyelids and a bad taste in my mouth and lack of energy.

Without too much information or really not that much concern I started CAPD. I was on that for two years. I coped with it quite well. I knew about dialysis and I didn't feel that my problem was life-threatening so I wasn't panicking about it. Also, I didn't get ill enough to feel vulnerable or incapable of taking care of myself. Believe it or not, it was more of an interesting experience for me. Because I've studied science and I've always been interested in science it was an opportunity to learn and see what was going on. I wasn't afraid to perform the treatment myself. I had to do five exchanges during the day and I did most of it overnight so that during the day I was free to do my work. I was tired but I was fortunate that my husband gave me and still gives me a lot of support. I was later informed that I was a candidate for a transplant.

What surprised me a great deal was that when I went on the list for a kidney transplant, I had this impression that it would be a minimum two-year waiting period. All of a sudden, however, three months after I went on the list, I was sitting at home watching Star Trek and the phone rang at 10 o'clock at night informing me that they had a kidney ready for me. I rushed to the hospital in a semi-daze. I got undressed, took a shower, and was sent to an operating room only to receive an unsuccessful kidney transplant. I did not have expectations of any kind since I had very little experience or preparation before the event. I learned that in some cases the kidney may not work for one or two weeks but may come to life afterwards. There were several patients with transplants whose kidneys had not started working yet. The lady who was in the bed beside me had kept a kidney for maybe three months and she was back in the hospital because her kidney was no longer functioning. There also was a man across the way whose kidney wasn't working. He appeared to be in bad shape but I later learned that his kidney started to work and he is fine. In my case, the doctor decided to remove the kidney after a week.

Gradually, over the summer, I recovered my strength and I was walking again. At that point, I felt that I couldn't cope with my job as principal of a school anymore. I had lost my will to work. Come September, I stayed home. At that point, I had another four years until retirement. In the meantime, even before the first operation, my sister had offered one of her kidneys without my knowledge. The doctors had found a white spot on her kidney and they told her that they were going to check it and do some more extensive testing to see if it was just some fat on the kidney or if there was some reason that she couldn't give me a kidney. She pressed the point that she wanted to be tested again. The doctor said that I had a very strong immune system which is probably why I rejected the first cadaver kidney and the only chance for success would be a with a transplant from my sister. There was a 25 percent chance that my sister and I would be completely compatible. My sister was tested and we were found to be 100 percent compatible. We chose the soonest possible time to have the transplant performed which I think took place February 23rd. I still didn't have any clear concept of what it would be like to have a transplanted kidney. In my mind, I imagined going from one state of feeling sick to another. I was assured that my quality of life would be much better but I didn't really understand what that meant. I didn't feel that I should take a kidney from my sister and I mentioned that to the doctor. He said that it was a gift which was given freely and that usually the donor gets more out of the gesture than the recipient because of the psychological or moral value of what they have done. I think it was easier to accept a kidney from my sister than from a stranger or even a friend.

My sister and I went to the hospital together. Her operation started one hour before mine. I woke up during the operation and a machine was breathing for me. As I tried to pull the tube out of my mouth, I became aware that a machine was helping me breathe. There were three or four residents assisting at the operation. I remember hearing one of them say that the kidney was already working. Apparently, the kidney had started working before they even attached it to the bladder. They said it was like a flood all over the floor. They noticed that I was awake and I remember them saying, "She's awake already". I went down to the recovery room where my sister was and we talked together. We both felt comfortable. Within the first 24 hours my new kidney had produced 24 liters of urine— a hospital record! Samples of my blood showed that my system had finally returned to normal after at least 20 years. I felt wonderful and within an hour after the operation I asked for a cup of coffee.

The transformation in my health was amazing. I felt better than I had in years. Before the operation, I could not imagine it possible that I could feel so good. I feel wonderful now and my sister is also fine, except she says that every time she hears the word "timber," she's afraid she's going to fall because she's like a tree that has been cut in half! My mother died not too long before the first transplant. My sister was living with my mother and they were each other's companion. Now my sister lives alone and we call each other more often.

Since the transplant, I take steroids and I have gained weight. I could eat constantly. I could get away with five or six hours of sleep a night and I still feel full of energy the next day. I'm also back at work. I go to the hospital every second month for a check-up and an adjustment in my medication. I feel that I will live a long and healthy life.

50

Christina, a 43-year-old woman, began treatment 32 years ago. Her treatment has been hemodialysis and two kidney transplants.

I was 11 years old when I was diagnosed with renal problems. This was in 1964. I was told that my problem actually started at birth because of problems with urination. From 11 to age 13, I was put on diets and just watched as to how things progressed because dialysis at that time was very new and it was not one of the options. But when I was 13 it became one of the options. My parents were asked if they would consider me going on hemodialysis and they said yes. My mother always tried to make things as normal as possible so I wouldn't feel abnormal in any sense, although I always felt a little bit out of the ordinary. I know that feeling was always there. Of course, kids at school couldn't understand why I wouldn't do gym. I was basically a loner in elementary school until I reached high school, so it kind of affected me that way. But other than that I think that I was a basically normal person. I helped around the house and I loved to color and do a lot of drawings and sew doll clothes which marked the beginning of my artistry. That kind of kept me sane even as a little girl.

Before the hemodialysis, I remember two things. Peritoneal dialysis was tried on me but it wasn't successful and I received a severe infection. Being a child this was very scary. Also, I started bleeding. I vomited blood and it was coming from every end that you can imagine except through the ears. It was really very frightening. I didn't know what was going on. Being a Roman Catholic and believing in prayer, I started singing a little prayer song that I learned in school. It made me feel better and gave me some courage when everyone was running around trying to take care of me to make sure that I didn't die. Once the blood stopped coming out from everywhere, I was rushed to another hospital and that's when they put me on hemodialysis.

I was on hemodialysis for two years and in the meantime I was going to school. I had to have many accesses. I had many operations because they would get blocked or infected. I was in and out of the hospital a lot. This caused me to be put back one year.

At age 15 I received a phone call and the doctor asked me if I was ready for a transplant because they had one ready for me. It was an exciting and scary time. I wondered whether it would be good or bad. But being 15 I was excited and wanted some normality. When I had my transplant it was also a surprise because my godparents came down from Mississauga to visit me. At that time you were put in a single room. You were very isolated. Anyone coming to visit you had to wear the full isolation garb with the hats, the masks, and the boots. I was in a room that overlooks the mountain and the cross from the mountain. I was very groggy because I was just coming out of the anesthesia after the transplant. I saw one large figure and one small figure coming towards me. Uncle Steve is 6'2" and Aunt Nellie is 4'9". I didn't recognize them because I was groggy. I asked them, "Are you angels? Did I die?" It's because it was dark and I could see the cross from the window. My aunt Nellie fainted and my uncle had to take her out of the room. I was thinking that angels don't faint! It was a little bit of a comedy situation. The transplant was a success and I was really grateful for that.

What I wasn't grateful for was finding out that when you take prednisone and immunosuppressants you gain a lot of weight. I ballooned up. Your self-esteem goes down. It was a hard thing to go through. The kids didn't understand and I was called lots of names. I was called the rock of Gibraltar. A lot of times I would look at the kids and say, "You don't really understand so it doesn't really bother me." But it did. I had two really good friends, Micheline and Louise. We were called the three musketeers. They knew that I had kidney problems. We used to go to parties and dances. I felt much more sane because I was having a normal life. I was very grateful to my two closest friends.

It was a good thing to have had the transplant. It gave me some normality but there were some complications. Two months into the transplant I developed a pulmonary embolism. I had phlebitis in my legs. I had to be put on medication intravenously and then orally. I was monitored for a long time until the clots in the lungs would disperse. Once or twice I had to have a boost because the kidney had minor rejections. After that it was okay. In the meantime, I graduated school. I met a really nice fellow and lived with him for two years. It was the first love of my life. I realized that I could have a life.

I stopped taking my antirejection medication. I didn't see my doctor for three years. I didn't have any blood tests done. I was living the life which I thought was that of a normal person. I eventually went back to the hospital because I was starting to feel crappy. The doctor didn't chastise me but explained to me why I should be taking my pills. He told me that my kidney was rejecting. In 1979, they didn't have all the things that could be done now. If the kidney blocked then that was it. Now they could put in a catheter or a "double J" to keep the place open so you can urinate. So I lost the kidney when I was 25. I had a very severe breakdown after that. I was depressed for at least three months. I felt guilty. I wondered why did this have to happen to me. Slowly I started to feel better when I was put back on hemodialysis. I found out later that part of my depression was caused by the toxins in my system. I made sense of it later but then I felt I was useless. I was scared. I thought that's it! No more transplant. No more life. But that's not so. I have a life. I have a good life. I have good nurses and doctors that take care of me. I have a good family and I have good friends. But I didn't see all of that back then. I want people to know that they have a chance. I was on hemodialysis for four years, from 1979 to 1983. A nurse suggested that I look into self-care dialysis. I was against it because I still wanted to wallow in my misery. But the nurses gave me information and I figured if other people can do it, I can too. I was taught how to operate the equipment. The hardest thing was needling myself. I had a fistula in my left arm. But it was hard. But somehow God was with me. I did a sort of hypnosis where I didn't think my arm was my own. I was also working at the time I was on self-care. It was ideal because my work was close to the dialysis center. Most of the time I worked regularly.

I was called to get another transplant. Unfortunately, the second transplant was more difficult. I had severe infection right after the transplant. It didn't work for two weeks after I received it. I had to be on hemodialysis. For a good six to eight months I had to have constant nursing care to treat the infection. I was happy to have the transplant because it was working but it disfigured my body. I was afraid that I wouldn't be accepted by the opposite sex because it really looked bad. I learned that if someone really cares about you it doesn't matter if you have scars, if you're fat, if you're sick. The person that loves you will love you no matter what.

I kept this kidney for 13 and a half years. Life was fairly good. When I was 31, I got an apartment. I was scared to live alone in case anything happened but I had to overcome my fear. I got a nice little place, elevator and all, and some good-looking guys which kind of convinced me! My health started deteriorating about five years ago in 1991. I wanted the doctors to do whatever they could to save my kidney which is what they tried to do. In the final stages, my doctor kind of sprang it on me that it was failing and that I would have to go back on hemodialysis. At that point, I already kind of knew.

When the doctors told me that they were going to put a permcath in my neck or shoulder, I told them to go ahead with it. When I was finally hooked up on hemodialysis, I was actually grateful because I was feeling so sick at that point. I was weak and every day was such a chore, such a challenge. I kept thinking that people who are waiting for a liver or heart transplant don't have anything to help them. We, as kidney patients, should feel privileged to have something to fall back on and prolong our lives until the next transplant.

You can't keep worrying about the medication and if it's working. How come I have a headache? Is my blood pressure too high? I do this to myself sometimes. Having a hobby stops you from all this crazy thinking. I try to have a positive attitude. It's not always easy. A lot of anger and frustration is in me that I have to watch out for. When I'm feeling really sick and lousy, sometimes I can't control my emotions and I get nasty. I try to keep that at bay but sometimes everything is going wrong.

All in all I do have a positive attitude. The doctors, the nurses, and the transplant team are great. They are sweet. Most of them take the time to listen even if they are busy. They give their best. I think good family, good friends, and excellent care gave me the strength to be here at 43 years old. Otherwise, without all of that I could have been gone a long time ago. I still have many things to do in this life. I want to do some more crocheting and maybe open up my own business. Who knows?

There is a lot of literature for the person who is unaware and scared to make themselves more familiar. Knowledge will help that person. Knowledge opens your mind and betters your understanding and then you don't feel so scared. Patients can always have their say. If they don't like something or don't want something done they can voice it. Maybe it will be explained to them better and then they'll understand better. A lot of times people are scared to say no but you're allowed. I've developed deadening of the nerves in the extremities and a possible heart condition. I'm hoping that it's all reversible. Again, one day at a time.

51

A 81-year-old man who wishes to remain anonymous began hemodialysis five years ago.

First of all I had a big operation, then they told me that I had to go on dialysis on account of my sickness. I could not do dialysis at home because I could not go through the operation needed. This was on account of my heart attack which happened only one month before. The next best thing was hemodialysis. I am very happy it happened this way. Being on hemodialysis I get out three times a week and talk with staff and patients, and in my condition these are my outings. It was very hard at the beginning and it's still hard now. It's hard because you can't go any place. You come home on Friday and you are really tired when you are finished. You have to rest, and the next day you can't go out, then it's Sunday, and then Monday, and the next thing you know you have to come back. The hardest thing about dialysis for me is, and it might sound stupid, but it's sitting down for three, four hours. I used to go out a lot, I was always out, then I couldn't go out anymore.

Dialysis has changed my life a lot. I used to play golf everyday, I liked it a lot. I had to give up some things. In my spare time I look at the TV, I watch sports a lot. At home I play cards, I play cribbage and "500". I have a cousin who comes to visit me twice a month, and we play cards, but when I am tired we stop.

The diet does bother me. I cannot eat my usual foods. I had to get used to eating food without salt, and I became restricted with my desserts and liquids, such as juice and water.

I would tell new patients that you have to make up your mind once they tell you that you have to be on dialysis. Me, I made up my mind right away, what's to be done, has to be done. Also, I try to take one day at a time, and after a week or two on dialysis there is little change. You should always hope for the best.

My wife is a pain in the neck, she watches me very closely, but she is a big help, she's the best. I live like a king. She was always like that. I have a driver who picks me up at 1:30 and my three children take turns picking me up at 6:00. I used to drive by myself, but two years ago I had an accident on account of a small stroke, so I cannot drive my car anymore.

I haven't got many friends, I have two friends for 50 years, and I told them about my dialysis. My best friend says to me, "When are you going to be cured?" I say, "I will never be cured." He was very surprised. With advanced therapy for my condition, I could be stable and live a few years more, which would make my wife very happy too.

52

Faustino Fererra, a 65-year-old man, began treatment 14 years ago. His treatments have been hemodialysis, peritoneal dialysis and a kidney transplant.

Once when I was working, I cut myself and I developed an infection and was given penicillin. It was at that point that my kidneys completely collapsed. I started hemodialysis but found it intolerable. I underwent six cardiac arrests while on hemodialysis! Two or three times, I had to be put on a respiratory machine to get me to breathe. When I had tuberculosis, I had one lobe from my lungs taken out. I believe that is what caused me to have all those cardiac arrests because I did not have enough oxygen in my lungs.

I suffered a lot while I was on hemodialysis and I had to stop this treatment. I then started peritoneal hemodialysis which worked well for me. I continued this treatment for about two years. Finally, I was lucky that they had a kidney ready for me to be transplanted. It has been 12 years since the transplant. Everything has been going smoothly ever since. I became diabetic, however, and I had to start taking insulin or I would have lost the kidney. I get scared when my sugar levels rise.

My family was happy when I had my transplant because they knew how much I had suffered in the past. So far, I am happy because now I feel good and everything is going well.

53

André Diochon, a 40-year-old man, began treatment 17 years ago. His treatments have been hemodialysis, three kidney transplants and a liver transplant.

The spring of 1975 I was enrolled in a police technology program. I had always dreamed of being a police officer. I would then get a law degree, and after a 20- or 25-year career, take my pension and practice law. It seemed like a reasonably good plan.

Over the fall and winter of 1975 I had a good part-time job. A routine medical found that I had protein in my urine. I was kept on my job while further medical tests were performed. I was then referred to a local hospital. By 1976 I was diagnosed with chronic renal failure, the disease being polycystic kidneys. I had to have periodic blood tests to determine the progression of my disease.

I knew then that the future I dreamed of would be lost. I didn't react well to that news. It was as if the rug had been pulled out from under my feet. I was stunned! I was hurt and confused enough not to realize that there were still options open to me. I was jealous of other young people who would be able to realize their dreams, and felt sorry for myself. I was not a violent or rough person growing up, but rather normal. I suddenly changed. While I played intramural sports I would try to inflict the pain and hurt I was feeling upon others.

In 1978 I was still feeling low. At a party for my boss I knowingly mixed pot, beer and blood pressure medication. I knew it was stupid, yet I was self-destructive. I ended up in an emergency room with terrible abdominal pain, a fractured jaw, and a severe concussion. I had fainted and fallen into a table. A couple of months later I got out of the hospital.

By the fall of 1979 my blood values had deteriorated to the point that dialysis was imminent. It hit me hard for two reasons; firstly, I didn't feel that bad physically, and secondly, I believed that I would receive a transplant from a cadaver and never need to be dialyzed. I was so confident that I didn't accept the kidney that had been offered to me by my brother.

I had visited a dialysis unit each time blood needed to be drawn. I know now that I was afraid of the process, despite the fact that I had spoken to a dialysis patient who had been receiving treatment for years. The dialysis machine that I would be treated with was a Travenol, a monster of a machine. It reminded me of a washing machine, whereby the dialysate was mixed with water in a large plastic tub, the mixture was pumped up into a basin in which a coil (artificial kidney made of porous cellophane type material) was placed. This resulted in a very hard dialysis. The amount of blood outside the system couldn't be controlled and the fluid removal was not precise. After each treatment I suffered from severe headaches, cramping and sometimes retching.

I became bored and I worried that I was just living from day to day. I decided to see an academic advisor. I chose to go to university. Only one problem remained; it would take me an hour and a half to get to school from home or from the hospital by bus. With treatments of at least five hours, my course selection and schedule were very limited. I also had a fear of taking care of myself on dialysis, although it was an option that was encouraged.

I needed to transfer to the hospital in downtown Montreal, but there were no places available. I was advised to transfer to a veterans hospital that was being closed, with the self-care dialysis unit absorbed by the hospital. The operative word in this scenario was "self-care". I would be responsible for my care which meant putting the needles into my fistula...a fate worse than death, but I wanted to go to school, and so I transferred. I arrived for my training with the attitude that I was going to learn as much as I could about dialysis. Putting needles in my arm was not as traumatic as I thought and in fact, the self-care environment liberated me. I became further implicated in my own care and I interacted with my doctors on a more equal footing. I found it empowering.

The weekend after my training finished, in August of 1984, I received the call. It was what I had hoped for—a kidney! I walked out on my balcony, it was sunny, I fought back the tears while each leg wanted to go its shaky way. The surgery went well. The transplant, however, did not. It was first diagnosed as ATN (acute tubular necrosis). That wasn't it though, I had the dreaded cytomegalovirus. I began to feel poorly and down. The transplant had to be removed, and I needed heart surgery because of a build-up of fluid in my heart. I was terribly sick and depressed. I requested the transplant psychiatric service. I thought that I was going out of my "nuts" mind. The psychiatrist reassured me that the simple fact of me asking him if I was "nuts", indicated that I was okay. I continued to see him post-transplant, to sort out a variety of issues. One issue was related to the fact that I had known that the donor of the kidney was female, and I had made a pact, while in the hospital, that I would have a family in order to ensure that her legacy would continue. I was engulfed in guilt about not keeping the transplant and therefore not upholding her legacy.

Going back on dialysis wasn't that difficult, since I was happy to be alive after the disaster I had just passed through. Self-care was some of the medicine I needed. I had lost faith in the transplant team, since I had relinquished much control of my life to them and I felt that they did not act in my best interests at the time. I was able to have a better relationship with my kidney doctors simply because I had more control of my care. After several months I became more alert and aware of my surroundings. A spate of patients began receiving transplants. At first I was jealous. Why were they getting organs while I was just sitting here years after a transplant almost killed me? Then it struck me, yeah, I can wish for a transplant for myself, but it was better to feel good for those lucky enough to have an opportunity to lead a normal life, free of the mechanical beast, which was my kidney. I then requested that I be put back on the transplant list.

Almost two years had passed since my first transplant and I was beginning to feel that opportunity had passed me by. In August of 1986 I was on dialysis studying for a summer course when a nurse and a doctor came to me and said that I was probably going to get another transplant and that it would be sometime between that evening and the next day.

I was so cool, or perhaps it was experience. By this time I had had a bilateral nephrectomy, transplant, transplant nephrectomy, and a pericardiectomy. I was no stranger to surgery. The next morning I finished showering, hopped on the gurney and went off to surgery. It went well, and it was working. I felt fantastic. I wanted to get out of the hospital, get back to school and get my life into gear. Then the transplant began to reject. My urine output dried up, my doctor took a biopsy to confirm rejection and he ordered some antirejection medication. I was feeling desperate, I could taste freedom. Fortunately the medication worked like a charm and I began to urinate again.

The most remarkable experience of having a transplant was eating a normal diet again. It wasn't the fact that my diet was restricted, but the sensation of feeling the nutrients flowing throughout my body. I could feel my body being replenished with energy, it was an incredible experience.

Once free of the hospital I returned to a regular life. However, what was normal (after all it had been seven years since I had gone to the bathroom), was how good I felt. I would ask people if this is what it felt like. They couldn't answer since they had never had a catastrophic illness and it is not something you sit down and think about. The transplant worked well, sort of... it lasted 16 months before it gave out. When I was told that it was over and that my chances of a cadaver transplant were between slim to none, tears flowed from my eyes without emotion. A silent sorrow. I hated returning to dialysis. It was horrific. I recovered from the initial period of feeling sorry for myself and would accept dialysis but only after I evaluated all my options.

I was now faced with doing something that I didn't do almost 10 years before; ask my brother for one of his kidneys. It took me a while to summon up the courage, but eventually I phoned him. I said to him, "Ten years ago you offered me your kidney, is that offer still good?" Inside I felt tension, not a fear of what his answer might be, but that I was asking someone to make the ultimate sacrifice; take a part of their body and give it to me. I was choosing to live with hope, or surviving with little or no hope on dialysis. Granted it is better to be alive on dialysis than to be dead. My brother, who had felt bad for me since I was receiving dialysis treatments, and wanted the best for me, was willing to donate his kidney, but he needed to check a few things out for himself. For example he had to make sure that his health would not be jeopardized, and more importantly that his family would be taken care of in case something would go wrong. He had to verify that the company he was working for would be in agreement, and that his wife would be part of the decision-making, as it would affect her and their children. It was all right, I would get my transplant. The wheels were put into motion. He was to have a medical evaluation and bloods were drawn to test our compatibility. May 25th, 1988 the surgery was performed successfully.

It has been close to nine years now. Since then I have also received a successful liver transplant.

Through all my treatments it is the unsung heroes to whom I owe so much. My family as well as my friends have absorbed my pain and frustration, silently suffering, while protecting me through their example. I now understand more about what love is.

Clara Guerra, a 66-year-old woman, began hemodialysis six years ago.

Before I started dialysis treatment I often went to see my doctor who was monitoring my diabetic condition. Gradually I began to feel weak and became swollen. The doctors determined that I was suffering from kidney failure and recommended that I start on dialysis treatments as soon as possible. I had no choice and so I started dialysis and I have never regretted my decision.

When the doctor told me that I must start dialysis, I felt discouraged and depressed because I had to come to the hospital three times a week for treatment. But with time I felt better and coming to the hospital so frequently didn't bother me anymore. Before dialysis I had been very sick and I couldn't move or walk because I was all swollen. After a while on dialysis I had lost about 60 pounds, all liquids that I had retained, and I regained my energy. I had not felt this well in a long time.

The diet for dialysis was almost the same as for my diabetes so I had no problems with that. On the other hand, I found it a little harder to live with the limits set on liquids because I am diabetic and I'm always thirsty. I sleep often during the dialysis because I can find nothing to do during the four hours of treatment.

My family always encouraged and helped me greatly during my illness. I would like to live a long time to see my grandchildren grow up. The nurses and personnel at the dialysis clinic are very kind and most encouraging.

My life hasn't really changed with dialysis. I still do the things I used to do before, but I do them just a little more slowly. Sometimes when I finish my dialysis and feel well enough I do my errands. Occasionally I even go out to walk. Unfortunately, I can't walk too far because my legs are weak and can't support my weight.

I look around at those who are sicker than I am and I feel so lucky. Other people have incurable diseases, but at least there is a cure for my illness and I continue my treatments because they make me feel much better. It's possible that I will ask for a kidney transplant but I must wait until an ulcer on my foot is healed.

To those suffering from kidney disease, I encourage them to take dialysis treatments because it's the only way to resolve those problems. At the start I was a little nervous about dialysis because I didn't know what it entailed, but once I got started I felt less apprehensive and began to feel much better. Don't worry about it because your health will improve and more importantly, it will prolong your life.

55

Arnaldo Romani (1922-1997) received hemodialysis for three and a half years.

Three years ago I was hospitalized to undergo an operation of the aorta, which had become swollen at the abdomen level. It was then that the doctor told me that they had discovered that one of my kidneys had ceased to function entirely and the other one had lost 75 percent of its effectiveness. I was then referred to the hospital because they had an excellent program there for kidney disease treatment. After the blood tests, the doctor confirmed the state of my kidneys and I was advised to start hemodialysis as quickly as possible because the kidneys had shrunk and had ceased to function.

During the first four months life was very hard for me. I always felt weak and vomited many times on the days of my dialysis. Once I got home I felt so tired I could do nothing. At the beginning I often became agitated because it was hard for me to accept both the illness and the dialysis. The other hardship for me was the restriction on what I could eat and drink. I love fruit and green vegetables, but the diet which I had to follow advised me not to eat a lot of potassium because it could affect the heart. Before I became ill I would have several beers with my friends after work. Now I can't drink at all because I must watch my liquid in-take. I like soup very much, but unfortunately I cannot have any as well.

All that I've talked about so far are the inconveniences of dialysis, but we shouldn't forget that without dialysis I could not have survived the last three years. When I have finished my treatment and leave the hospital I take small walks and try to forget about dialysis and think very positively. It's true that dialysis has made me do without many things that I like, but I say to myself, "Don't fret about things like beer and vegetables, Arnaldo, because you've tasted them all before and you mustn't fret too much if you can't do it anymore". Now that I've become used to my new kind of life everything is going very well. The days of my treatments I meet other Italians who are also getting dialysis treatments and in talking with them the time passes quickly. I also feel lucky as well, because there are many other people that suffer and die from other incurable diseases. At least I have the dialysis machine available to me which allows me to live longer and I don't think I should ask for more than that.

56

A 56-year-old man who wishes to remain anonymous started hemodialysis four years ago.

I have been on dialysis for four years. My doctor asked me what type of dialysis I preferred and I chose to have hemodialysis. My doctor was checking the blood every three or four months and the last time they found out that I had to go for hemodialysis.

Nothing has changed but it's not like before when I was working. Every two weeks you receive your pay but now you are no longer making money. I used to work full time but now I can't work. I can't work because after I come off from the machine I feel so tired. When I go back home after dialysis I feel so tired and I have to sleep for at least half an hour. Before I liked to eat a lot of fruits but now there are certain fruits I can't eat because they have too much potassium. Now I watch a little bit of TV and I spend time relaxing. If I feel better, I try to clean the house a little bit. I accept this. What can you do? You can't do better than that.

I'm married and I have two sons who are both going to school. One has a part-time job and one is still at home. My wife and my kids give me support. I'm interested in getting a transplant and I expect to have one in the future. After I would like to go back to work but it depends on how well you feel.

57

Sandra Buraglia Pinard, a 51-year-old woman, began treatment four years ago. Her treatments have consisted of peritoneal dialysis, hemodialysis and a kidney transplant.

I was told by a doctor that I have this hereditary kidney disease in my family, and that I should go check it out. I had some sort of x-ray, but it came out negative, so I was happy. The next thing I knew, my oldest brother had kidney disease, and Doug was on dialysis for 11 years before he passed away. Another brother, Claude, had it. He lived out in California, and he was on dialysis but he got a transplant. I have another brother who lives in the Maritimes and he was on dialysis at the time, but he also had a transplant. My oldest sister, also in Halifax, was on dialysis. My brother in Halifax was looking for a kidney and I spoke to his doctor, and told him that I would be glad to go for tissue testing to see if I could give him a kidney, but we didn't match. However, I did match with my older sister Rita. Her doctor contacted me to find out if I wanted to donate a kidney and I said, "Yes". I came in for donor evaluation, and the first test I went through was an ultrasound. About four hours later my doctor came up to see me and said, "I'm sorry but you won't be giving a kidney to your sister." So sure that I had nothing wrong with my kidneys, the only thing on my mind was that I had cancer. He said, "No, you have polycystic kidneys." So in that way I started being followed at this hospital.

At first I came into the hospital once a year, then it got to be once every six months, and then it got to be a bit closer together. I had my fistula in August, and in December 1992 I went on hemodialysis. They are a very caring group of people that are in dialysis. It's a whole new type of people. They very calmly walk you through every little step, and if I didn't want to look, I didn't have to. I went into self-care and I thought I was doing really good, but on the last day in May my fistula blocked. I was put on dialysis through an artery in my groin. I went back for another operation to unblock the fistula and when I came out of the surgery I had a tube in my stomach. CAPD dialysis was explained to me, and that was what I had to do. For CAPD dialysis you don't come to the hospital. The CAPD group showed me how to do it myself for about a month before I started, during which time I received dialysis through the artery in my leg.

If you compare the two, CAPD is better time-wise, but if you want to relax more, in hemodialysis you are at the hospital and you are relaxed. Dialysis for me was not hard in any way, shape or form. The only thing I found with hemodialysis is that you have to come here to the hospital. But then again, when you are here, everybody else is in the same boat. When I was on hemo I wasn't sick, but it does take over your life. That's all you think of. So I would say, "Well this day, count it out because I'm going on dialysis, I can do something on Tuesday, but forget Wednesday, Thursday is okay, but forget Friday." When you are on CAPD it's different, you are at home doing it, you can go visit someone as long as you take the medication you need with you. The only thing I found with the hemo is that I had to come here to the hospital, but it became a social event. It's true, I came in here for three hours, three days a week and I saw the same people, and they became my friends. You sat down  and talked to them and that was the social event of the week, you say, "Hey, I'm going to see them on Monday, I'm going to see them on Wednesday..."

I had my name in for a kidney transplant, and I was only nine months waiting. I remember my sister saying, "It comes when you are not thinking about it." I remember it was 7:00 in the morning and I was sleeping when I got the call. I was at the hospital at 9:00 in the morning but the operation wasn't until 2:00 in the afternoon, so I can remember getting ready to run down to the dialysis unit, just to see everybody and to tell them that I was getting a transplant. I had absolutely no pain with regard to the transplant. In the same way you go into the hospital to have a baby, and you come out with something you didn't have when you came in, it's a joyous operation.

58

Margot Matthews Keith-King (1942-1995) began treatment 15 years ago. Her treatments were hemodialysis and a kidney transplant.

Margot's creativity gave her the ability to express herself both through the written word and illustrations. Margot provided original drawings for "dial.log", a newsletter for dialysis patients, of which she was co-editor.

The following letter was written to Peter Gzowski host on CBC Radio's cross-Canada program, "Morningside". It was written in response to a request for stories about personal experiences with computers for a series of programs on computers.

Mr. Peter Gzowski, "Morningside"
CBC Radio
P.O. Box 500, Station "A"
Toronto, Ontario M5W 1E6

Well Peter,

Let me tell you about <u>my</u> computer. We have a kind of love/hate relationship, although I must admit most of the emotion exists on my side. We have what might be termed a "forced marriage" and it entails much ambivalence on the part of the bride: me. You see, my computer is a kidney dialysis machine. We first encountered each other about a year and a half ago. At the beginning I was very passive, frightened and resentful. We communicated only with the intercession of a nurse.

Last fall, I transferred to a self-care dialysis unit and learned to program my computer myself. It began to seem a little bit friendlier. I mastered the workings of a rhodial machine, a handsome-looking fellow enameled cobalt blue. Shortly after becoming familiar with his dials and buttons and flashing lights, he was supplanted by a sleeker and jazzier young computer going by the name of "monitral". Now this is some machine! It is user-friendly. It has soft rubber buttons to cushion my fingertips. It has little phrases under each dial and light to tell me if there is air in my bloodlines. It tells me the amount of dialysate I have in my tank, the temperature of this fluid, the speed of the blood pump, you name it! It talks too. That is, it has little gold lights, green lights and red lights that shine to point out different bits of information and it also "beeps" warnings to me if anything is going wrong. This is not too bad for a machine. It really does encourage a personal relationship. I often make little sniping remarks at my monitral when it beeps excessively and have been known to give it an occasional kick. I am not alone in this. Fellow patients and hospital staff also talk to and threaten various dialysis machines.

Of course, the crux of this relationship is the utter dependency of it. I would not be alive if it were not for the blood-cleansing efforts of my monitral. It is very difficult to realize that this is true and even then, to accept it. Thus the ambivalence. I am still fairly young and may someday have a chance for a kidney transplant, but until then my computer and I are a team, three days a week, four hours at a clip and no holidays!

Best wishes, Peter.

Margot's art work is included with the permission of
Richard Matthews and Sandra McCallum.

The Typist

** This illustration appears in "dial.log"
(a newsletter for dialysis patients) as a
thank-you to a nephrology secretary who
typed the text.*

59

Suzanne Doré, a 51-year-old woman, began hemodialysis three years ago.

When I first found out that I had to begin dialysis, I was given a choice among different types of dialysis treatments, and I chose hemodialysis. I chose it because I'm a very social person, and being on hemodialysis allows me to come to the hospital and see a lot of people. I also find it helpful to see other people who are in the same situation as I am, because then I do not complain as much. I live alone, so when I come to the hospital I am so glad to see all the other people, and I care for them. It's like a big family.

At the hospital, everyone is so supportive of me. During my first year of dialysis, I was sick and I had a hard time. At the hospital, I'm not a number, I'm a person. The personnel is wonderful, and I love all of them. Maybe that's why I am feeling so great today! I feel wonderful inside and out. It seems to me as though when I feel good inside my head, my body simply follows.

So now, I still have all my friends that I had before the treatment, and I also have the new friends that I made in dialysis. They are all very supportive. I also have a son, and he has been very supportive of me as well. I try not to rely on him too much, because he is a student and he is busy. But he does his best, and he often calls me to see if I need anything. So I am very happy all over, because of the way in which things are working out. Before starting dialysis, I did not know how things would turn out, and I was worried as to what the outcome would be. But now, I think, why worry? I take things one day at a time, and I do my best. I follow the doctors' orders, and I watch my diet. This helps me to feel better.

During the time that I have been on dialysis, my attitude towards dialysis has changed a lot. Before I began, I did not like the idea of having to come to the hospital three times a week. It took a few months for me to accept that I really need this treatment in order to stay healthy and have a normal life. I think that it is important for people on dialysis to accept their condition and to look on the bright side of things. I know that there is nothing that I can do by myself to make my kidneys better, and that I need the help of the treatment for that. Being on dialysis has also helped me to become more patient, because it has taught me to sit for three or four hours straight without moving. This was difficult at first, but now I really do not mind it anymore.

Actually, my life has become better since I began dialysis, because now I feel like doing things. For example, if there is a wedding, I can accept the invitation. I go out to see shows, and I go out with my son. It's like a whole new life! I feel good, and I accept that there are some limitations in my life. I know that there are certain things that I cannot do as quickly as I used to, such as cleaning my house. But what I cannot do today, I simply do tomorrow. I have also learned to accept help from people who offer it, which is something I had difficulty doing before. I used to be too proud, and I thought that I could do everything by myself.

It is true that I have been through a lot. But I try to stay positive, and I tell myself that I will get well. I tell myself that tomorrow will be better than today, and this is what usually happens. I think that the reason for this is that a person's mind can really affect the healing process. I was very sick for several months, and I had to stay in the hospital for a long time. But I came out of it, and it is hard to express how wonderful I feel now. If I ever get sick again, I will simply take the same approach. I will remain positive, and put all my best efforts into getting well. I have always been a fighter, and I think that it is important to always keep a good attitude.

I also have a strong faith that not only will I not be sick in the future, but that there will be a time where no one will be sick. I am a Jehovah's Witness, so I believe that this is true according to the Bible. This helps me too, and it keeps me going every day. I believe that one day, the world will be changed, and there will be no more kidney disease. Due to that, I get up in the morning with a smile, and that keeps my hope and my smile strong throughout the day.

60

Mr. Desgroseilliers, a 66-year-old man, has been on hemodialysis intermittently since 1990 and continuously for the past year.

Not so long ago I was like the "Car of the Year", with a V8 motor and able to do 100 mph without difficulty. Everything seemed permissible and I deprived myself of nothing. I was a hard worker so I deserved to own many things and since money flowed in easily, I had no problems. Problems, that was for others, those who found it hard to keep up with me. I participated in several sports, such as hunting in far off places and fishing in rough waters, and I liked to talk about my exploits to everyone who liked to be thrilled. I loved risk, and taking precautions against the cold, the bad weather and overwork, that was for others, not me. All that was about 10 years ago.

One weekend in June 1990, everything started to happen: red patches all over my body, vomiting. Monday, I was at the emergency in a pitiful state. After tests were done it was found that my urea level was abnormally high and I was sent for dialysis. From then on I started going for regular dialysis treatments. At the same time my daughter undertook to give me osteopathic treatments in order to re-establish function in that part of my kidneys that was still healthy. This improved my condition to the point that the dialysis was discontinued, under medical supervision. I was very happy then, since I thought that I was now out of the woods and able to get rid of dialysis.

This state of affairs was upset suddenly one year ago. Following a small accident, a fall, the urea level in my blood was found to be high and my red corpuscle count was low. So I had to restart dialysis treatments three times a week. I was always tired and out of breath, and with the slightest exertion anemia would show up, and possibly edema.

Now I have become sensible, or at least that's what I think, since I am waiting for a kidney donor. I'm done with mourning for perfect health, overdoing things, foolishness. I know that I can live with this for a long time and that I am the first and most important one responsible for looking after my health. And yet, there are moments when I would love to put my kidneys on my doctor's desk and tell him to do anything he wants to mend them. While this was happening, I would go on holiday and on my return I would take back my mended kidneys. Then I could use them to go hunting, fishing and traveling... maybe something like that will happen to me one day with a transplant, if someone who has taken good care of his kidneys would give me this invaluable gift. It is said that, "time and patience often do more than strength and courage". I've learned this, I've understood, I am thankful and I'm not waiting for the impossible, but for what is possible.

From the bottom of my heart I thank those who are expanding the frontiers of the possible, without quitting.

61

Robert Taylor, a 43-year-old man, began treatment two years ago. His treatments have been hemodialysis and peritoneal dialysis.

I found out that my kidneys were failing approximately four or five years ago. Being a diabetic, my endocrinologist noticed some fluid build-up. The doctor waited pretty much to the last moment in telling me that I would be going on dialysis. He said that I would be going on it in a year or so but I ended up going on it within a few months, so I really didn't have time to absorb the idea. The orientation, in my opinion, was very insufficient. It didn't answer the questions I wanted to know. In retrospect, I think that I kind of made a mistake in choosing hemodialysis at the time. I was on hemodialysis for almost two years. If I had the choice to do it all over again, I would have chosen CAPD because your overall health is better. You don't have the peaks and valleys that you have with hemodialysis. It's very stressful physically, emotionally, and mentally to have to come into the hospital three times a week. Whereas with CAPD your well-being is steady. It was very hard on my family life. My family is gone now. They couldn't take it. My children were feeling that I wasn't there for them and they weren't really understanding what I was going through. They don't really remember before I was sick. I had almost completely withdrawn within myself because I didn't want them to see the pain I felt. There's a lot of pain that goes with this. They were very unhappy, so one night they packed up and left. If it wasn't for my parents, sister and nieces and a few close friends who stood by me,

and of course Maria, my girlfriend of 14 years, I would never have survived this ordeal. And of course, my social worker, who endured hours of ramblings.

On my birthday, October 27th, I was called in for a transplant and when I came in they found that I had a high fever and that my leg was infected because I had a small cut on my foot. Quite obviously, the transplant didn't go through.

I feel better now but my diabetes has skyrocketed since being on CAPD and it's very hard to control. Now that I'm on CAPD I'm happy to have more free time. I'm a musician and I play guitar, keyboard, and the saxophone. I can play music and work on the computer. It's not confining like hemodialysis. With hemodialysis you have a regimen where you have to come in at a certain time and you're put in a chair and you're sitting there... it's stressful. Actually, music has made me survive this. When I would get really down to a point where I couldn't take it anymore, I would lose myself in my music and that would bring me up again. I also like painting so I have things I can fall back on and it helps me get through it. I'm a very private person and it's very hard for me to go to my friends, go to my parents, or go to my siblings and tell them what I think. It's through necessity that I've had to talk more about my feelings and what has been going on inside of me. I would tell new patients to research their disease and to not be afraid to ask questions.

62

Mario Pion, a 37-year-old man, began treatment seven years ago.
His treatments have been hemodialysis and peritoneal dialysis.

My story is a bit different than others because I chose to combine peritoneal dialysis and hemodialysis at the same time. In between the days of my hemodialysis I do peritoneal dialysis. I am the only one amongst all those that I know under treatment that made this choice. It was simply the most efficient solution for me. I like to have a certain quality of life, and in combining these two methods of dialysis I can have more control over my diet. Above all, I can control my intake by using this system, although it's not something that is advisable for everyone.

I started on dialysis seven years ago. At the beginning, what helped my morale was that I was part of a group that was working to help people that were addicted to drugs. I drew a lot of personal energy from working with a group towards common goals. I continued to work at this during the first six months of my dialysis and during that time I put in between 12 and 18 hours a day. The fact that I was helping those people and saving their lives indirectly acted as a kind of therapy for me. I don't know what gave me such energy but I suppose it was the instinct for survival.

Before I started on dialysis I was in business and it was going extremely well but, afterwards, I had to make some changes. Before, I lived at 100 mph and burnt the candle at both ends. It was dialysis that made me realize that to live like that was overdoing it. Because of that I am more conscious of my well-being and so I've learned to take it easier, and it's mostly thanks to peritoneal dialysis which I have to do four times a day. It helps me to take time out and relax and as a consequence has brought another dimension to my activities.

The sources of my support most of all have been my wife, my family and those around me. Despite my desire to always be self-sufficient there are days when I lack the energy. Consequently, those around me must be extremely patient, principally my wife. I find the job my wife has done absolutely fantastic because in this kind of situation all attention is directed towards the patient and rarely towards those who are part of the support group. Those people who are constantly preoccupied with wanting to know how the patient is doing never seem to ask how the caregivers are feeling. My wife at times has found this hard to take because our friends don't remember to give credit where it is due. I think that they should be more aware of the great work being done by the spouse. My wife never leaves me even though sometimes she would like to let up a bit. Everything isn't always perfect and there are highs and lows, but one thing is certain; without those around me I doubt if my morale would be as good as it is.

For those just starting dialysis for the first time, I know that they are in an anxious state, as I had been at the start. The advice I can give them is to avoid anxiety at all costs because this can result in mental barriers. Dialysis didn't stop my life and I think you can get through this very well if you set your mind to it. Simply remind yourself to dole out your energies. I have remained active and what has given me strength is my inner aggressiveness. In the final analysis all this is part of surviving. We have no other choice and neglecting treatments is self-defeating. My attitude is not one of resignation, it is simply the means for survival.

63

A 76-year-old woman who wishes to remain anonymous began hemodialysis five months ago.

I was quite angry at first when I learned that I had kidney failure. I could not find any literature that would enlighten me. I did get a book from the hospital that had a lot of very good things in it. I thought that if I could contribute anything to this book then that would be good.

I was diagnosed with kidney failure on June 28, 1996. I don't know if it had to do with an angiogram that I had but this is what I was told. I was angry at first, very angry with everyone. I was telling them that I was all right. I couldn't believe it. I'm not angry now. You just have to make the best of it. Dialysis is something that I have to do and so I do it. I'm a Scorpio! At first, I didn't notice any changes when I started dialysis but my sons did. I used to rattle off a mile a minute and I was very impatient. I seem to have calmed down considerably. Dialysis has helped a great deal. You have your moments of weakness but I suppose that has to go with it. Since going on dialysis I haven't had to make any changes. I'm free to do as I please. I do light housework and I do all the cooking. I have everything done the day that I'm coming to the hospital because I always prepare something the day before. It's still a lot of work but I do it. That's my job.

A Few Good Tips

- *You can take little meals and if you are still hungry in the afternoon, take a bowl of puffed wheat or shredded wheat which is good for you with as little milk as possible.*

- *Keep your feet up because they swell. If I don't do it, my son comes over and puts the hassock under me to put my feet up.*

- *My son told me to take deep breaths while on dialysis because I break out in a sweat and I feel like I'm going to pass out, but before I do I get the nurse. Before this comes on I yawn and yawn, my nose gets ice-cold, and my pressure is low. I only had 10 minutes to go the other night and then it hit me but I called the nurse and she told me to lie back and I was okay in about a minute.*

64

Winston Cross began his treatment three years ago. His treatment has consisted of hemodialysis and a kidney transplant. Beverly Tweed donated her kidney to Winston.

Winston: I had kidney problems for 10 years before beginning dialysis. Eventually, my kidney function deteriorated to the point where dialysis was necessary. I had to start coming to the hospital for hemodialysis three times a week. I also had many restrictions as to what I could and could not eat, and I found this very difficult. Eventually, Beverly decided that she did not want me to go on like this anymore. She then undertook to donate one of her kidneys to me, but first she had to come to the hospital for a whole battery of tests to determine if we were compatible. It was revealed that she was suitable, and that we could proceed with the transplant. Beverly has Type O blood, which means that she is a universal donor.

Beverly: To me, there was never any real decision in giving Winston my kidney. I did that automatically, but the real difficult moment was when I had to go for all the tests and I did not know whether we would be compatible or not.

Winston: On December 13th of 1995, Beverly and I both came to the hospital for our respective operations. We were both lying on stretchers, and they came to take her to the operating room first. When I saw that, the tears came to my eyes. I could not understand how it was possible that I was the sick one, and yet they were taking her to the operating room. I could not believe that she was doing all this for me. Afterwards, we both woke up together in the recovery room, and she was in more pain than I was. As for myself, I did not understand what was happening, but all of a sudden I had the sensation that I needed to urinate. I had a catheter attached to me, but I did not know that. When the urine came into my bag, it was a sign that my kidney was working. At that point, I was told that everything was going to be alright.

Beverly: Right, I was released on the 22nd of December, and he was released on the 23rd. We wanted to go home together! Well, I went home first anyway. Then he came home, and I have not had a break since!

Winston: After the transplant, I went home and recovered nicely. Things were going well for us. The whole month of January was great. We both felt as if we had been given a second chance at life. After my transplant, I was very relieved that I did not have to go to dialysis anymore. I felt that I was free from the process of dialysis, and that I could finally function like a normal person. However, I was still feeling very tired, and at one point my temperature began rising so much that I had to be brought in to the hospital again. One day while I was there, I got up to go to the washroom, and all of a sudden my knees buckled under me and I fell to the floor. Someone picked me up, and I thought nothing more of it. But the next morning, I fell to the floor again when I got up to get weighed. After that, I was transferred to the Montréal Neurological Hospital.

Beverly: And I was so surprised because he had been doing well. However, at the time, I did not think too much of it myself. I thought, whatever it is, he's in good hands, and they're looking after him. Then, we received the diagnosis for his symptoms. It turned out that he had

Guillain-Barré disease, which is caused by a virus that enters the body and prevents the nerves from stimulating the muscles. This eventually leads to paralysis. However, there are more mild and severe forms of the disease, and Winston had it in a very severe form. In fact, it was the most severe case of it

they had seen at that hospital, which is saying a lot because they special-ize in treating that. Of course, I was not aware of that at the time, and if I had been, I probably would have run away screaming.

Winston: Actually, Beverly can pick up the story from here, because after this point I was just gone. I was not aware of what was happening to me anymore.

Beverly: Well, not right away. First, he was transferred to the Montréal Neurological Hospital. Then, things started to become progressively worse. Eventually, he could not move his legs because the disease was slowly climbing up his body, destroying the muscles one at a time. At that point, I was staying with him all the time and I was getting very little sleep. I had to be there for him because his skin was often itchy but he could not scratch it. So I had to scratch it for him.

Winston: I would wake up at three or four in the morning when I needed to scratch, and I was so grateful that she was there.

Beverly: But you know, I was also feeling very much in the way there. I got the feeling that some of the nurses thought I was in the way, and that I should not be there all the time. Yet, when I did leave to get a change of clothes or check on my apartment, Winston would tell me that he was just counting the minutes until I came back. I was absolutely torn between all the things I needed to do on the outside, and staying with him all time.

Winston: In any case, the rest of my story can be picked up by my doctor, who saw me come as close to the edge as possible and return from there. Eventually, the disease reached my lungs, and my condition deteriorated to the point where I had to be put on a respirator. I started bleeding profusely from my rectum, and my temperature rose to above 40° C. I was quickly brought to the intensive care unit, and I had to receive 12 liters of blood to compensate for all the blood I had lost.

Beverly: During this difficult time, we drew strength from each other and from within. I was constantly in the hospital, staying with him as much as I could.

Winston: I felt that I had to live, if only for Beverly. I was thinking of her all the time. Eventually, the disease reached my eyes too, and I did not even have enough strength to close them. There were times when I slept with my eyes open. I also could not chew anything, so my food had to be put in a blender. My whole body was in pain, and I was constantly shaking all over. Although this disease was unrelated to my kidney problems, I believe that it affected me because I had a lowered immune function after my transplant. One consequence of this experience has been that I now have a renewed appreciation for the time I am spending just being alive. Before, when a day would pass by, that was all it was to me—just another day gone by. But now, a day is much more precious to me than it was previously. I realize that I am not in total control, and that there is some type of power that controls everything. When I was in the hospital, I could not do anything for myself, and yet everything turned out well for me. I am now at the Montréal Rehabilitation Center, recovering from Guillain-Barré disease. Although my legs are not paralysed, I have very little muscle left in them and I am currently not able to walk. However, I am working very hard on that, because I want to walk again. Although doctors have told me that I will not walk again, I am working on it with my physiotherapist, and I am contributing my share to this team effort. Now, I no longer believe that there is anything in life which I really, really need. My health is what is most important to me. As for the rest, I am glad when things get done, but if something does not work out, I no longer become upset about it.

Beverly: As for myself, I am often with him at the rehabilitation center, to help him with anything he needs. It is not always easy, and I am very, very tired, but I simply take things one day at a time.

65

Rowland Rudd (1925-1997) was on hemodialysis for two weeks at the time he told this story.

I found out about my kidney problems after coming into the hospital for four weeks and going through tests everyday. I had very few medical problems until I was 70. Now I can't play golf, I can't drive a car, and I can't curl. I hate coming in here three times a week. Well, it's not that bad. I've had a pretty healthy life up to now, so I'm not used to going to the hospital. I did not know what dialysis was, but my wife found out about it. She is a big help to me. She handled it pretty well. She is my wife, my nurse, my cook. It was really hard for my daughter, my grandson and granddaughter, who were more upset then we were. They are very sensitive to my condition and very loving.

I hate the diet. I loved orange juice, I lived on it. I find the diet the most difficult part, but my wife says, "You can still have lots of things!"

In my spare time I like to write. I have a fantastic collection of magazines from England that were published primarily in the 1920s and 1930s. I still read them occasionally. The trouble is that I haven't really whacked away at my typewriter since this happened. I hope to come back to writing. I think this is something that can help me, if I could find the energy to do it. I am awfully tired these days. I take nine different drugs in the morning and the same at night. They are supposed to lower my blood pressure but they aren't helping.

66

A 74-year-old man who wishes to remain anonymous began hemodialysis 16 months ago.

I have been on dialysis for approximately 16 months. I was anxious to get on dialysis because I was feeling so bad. Going on dialysis is the best thing that has ever happened to me. Before I got on dialysis I was at a stage where I had to sit down to shave. It was a real chore. Within two sessions on dialysis I was really perked up.

This diet thing really bugs me, like no salt in my food. I still have to get used to that and I don't think that I ever will. I love to sit down and have a plate of fish and chips with vinegar and salt but that's a no-no. There is high potassium in potatoes. I can't have bananas, oranges, kiwis, pomegranates, everything that I like. I was eating all of these things and I was slowly killing myself because I wasn't aware of the potassium. The difficult part I think more than being on dialysis is trying to keep a diet. I cheat sometimes.

Coming in for dialysis is no big deal except that I can't go traveling when I want. I traveled occasionally including Barbados and England. Since I've been on dialysis I haven't been anywhere except on a country trip 100 kilometers away. After I'm finished dialysis sometimes I'm a little tired and the thought of driving all the way to the country is too much especially in the winter. The city has its conveniences but I prefer the country.

I have two boys and two daughters. At the present time I'm staying with a daughter of mine. My wife of course and my daughter with whom I'm staying with are a great source of support. When I had to go on dialysis, my family had been sort of prepared for it because I have a son that was on dialysis. He got a kidney transplant just before Christmas. We were both blessed with high blood pressure. In his case he went to Toronto for a job and when he was there he got involved with a charismatic church. They said God takes care of every human being. He got off the pills for his high blood pressure. He stopped taking his medication and for a while he was doing great and then it hit him. He came back to Montréal and found out that his kidneys were failing.

I'm retired from work. I've been retired for 14 years. But it didn't turn out the way I figured. I figured that when I retired I would do what I wanted when I wanted but then that's the luck of the draw. There are people who are worse off.

I attended a couple of meetings when I first got on dialysis for people who were going to start on dialysis or who have just started. I couldn't understand why people feared coming on dialysis because I was so sick. I could not wait to get on dialysis. After a couple of sessions I felt great. I would tell new patients to get on dialysis as soon as you can and try to stick to your diet.

My being here is my own fault. I really abused my body in my earlier days. I'd go out late at nights, staying out all night and then going to work. In the army I drank more than I should have. So I can't really complain. I could say that they should have given me different treatments but it's my fault.

I don't know if it will ever happen but I'm going on the transplant list. Maybe some old joker will kick the bucket. Maybe the kidney has 10 or 20 more years left in it. Old people could have good kidneys too. My wife's father was Irish and she's never been to Ireland. I thought that if I get a transplant then maybe next year we could go. Maybe we could go anyway and make arrangements for dialysis over there.

67

Jacqueline Poirier Payette, a 59-year-old woman, began treatment 17 and a half years ago. Her treatment has included hemodialysis and a kidney transplant.

In January 1959, I was 21 years old, married for only two years, seven months pregnant and deliriously happy when I was brought down by an illness so strange that medical science took more than 10 years to diagnose it.

After a very difficult delivery, on March 8th, 1959, I gave birth to a beautiful baby girl weighing seven and a half pounds, full of life and in good health. Unfortunately, the illness that had assaulted me three months earlier never left me. After I returned home the state of my health grew worse, I lost all confidence in myself and in my abilities. I was convinced that I was a bad wife, a bad mother, that I could not look after my home much less work at an outside job. I felt diminished, inhabited by a feeling of inferiority and powerlessness, which is why I then developed ulcerative colitis which only served to worsen my health.

During 10 long years I tried to find the cause of this idiopathic sickness which possessed me and prevented me from living a normal life. I didn't understand what was happening to me. I had always been an independent young woman, I had never been sick before. My first time in hospital had been for the birth of my daughter.

"The best way to heal yourself is to act as though you are healed". I became pregnant a second time, but in the fifth month of my pregnancy I lost the baby. When I had a therapeutic abortion it was found that the baby had been dead for some time. (I learned later that no baby could have survived given the state of my kidneys at that time).

I consulted many doctors, I was hospitalized several times, I even turned to alternative medicine, I did everything I could, but nothing worked. Because I looked frail, the doctors said that my sickness was a nervous condition... I believed that I was "mental" and I wanted to give up. "To lose hope is to die a slow death. But God exists. He heard my prayers, life took a new turn and I learned how to live again".

In 1968 a friend, my sister-in-law, took me to see a specialist in internal medicine at the Royal Victoria Hospital. This doctor, after having truly "listened" to me, understood my despair and really wanted to help me.

From that day on my life changed. I regained confidence, at last I had hope. I have since then considered this doctor a friend, and I have always called him "my Doctor Welby" (as in the American TV show). He has been my doctor for more than 25 years and I have never regretted it. He has been my advisor, through thick and thin.

On the day I first consulted him, this doctor assessed that I was sick enough to be hospitalized without delay. After I was subjected to an array of tests he came to me and said, "Since our interview several days ago you never mentioned your kidney disease. When did it happen?" I answered, "I have never had a kidney disease, I have never had any kidney pains. They must have given you the diagnosis for another patient". But unfortunately he was right! My kidneys were functioning at 25 percent of their capacity. I urgently needed intensive medical treatment and would probably have to undergo dialysis treatments in the near future.

It seemed that from my first pregnancy on I had been brought down by an attack of nephritis. Furthermore, following that, the medication that I took for my ulcerative colitis hastened the deterioration of my kidneys. I was suffering from a kidney disease called interstitial nephritis (with all that it implied). This hit me like a club! (Although I must admit finding out I was physically rather than mentally ill made me feel a lot better!).

From that day on I sought to learn by whatever means, as much as could be learnt about this infamous disease so as to cooperate to the limit in the treatments prescribed by my doctors.

When one sees things clearly one is better equipped to face them. Knowledge often alleviates fear, knowledge is power. I was thirsting for life and decided for myself, my daughter, my husband and all who loved me to do everything I could to get well. With the help of the nephrologist recommended by my doctor I was at last given appropriate treatments.

The good care I received delayed my dialysis treatments for about 10 years.

I had had a career that I loved, so while taking adequate medication and with the help of my doctors and husband I decided to start working again. Of course, it wasn't easy. At Radio-Canada where I had worked as a script assistant before my illness, the doors were closed to me when it was found that I was suffering from a chronic illness and I was turned away. It was the same story in all the "big" companies.

Thus, looking in other directions, I went freelance in the fields of communications and public relations; fields in which I excel and in which I am trained. Very often working hours were irregular, frequently at night and on weekends, and this made my scheduled visits to the hospital easier. I learned very quickly, at my expense, that I could never tell my clients that I was suffering from a chronic illness. At that time, I started to live a double life. I had two agendas; a professional and a medical one.

When I was being interviewed, I never mentioned having a kidney ailment. My employers only discovered it after I had proved my worth, either months or years later. I never spoke of it, I did not appear sick, I looked after my appearance and I was seldom absent from work. Migraines, headaches and minor ailments were never sufficient justification for me not to show up.

During my dialysis I left the office at three p.m. and didn't get home until about 10 p.m. When I had my transplant operation, I was absent from work for only three months. As a press agent I always took work with me to the hospital to try to make up the two hours of work I lost, twice a week. In any case, at the time I had a rather difficult employer who used to say, "I hope you have carefully studied the manuscript on which you have to work. You really have to make up for the two hours of work that you lose during your dialysis". I must tell you that I often dreamt of "plugging" him into the (dialysis) machine, he and others like him. But "one must forget the past and leave the future to Providence." (Bossuet)

I remember that before my dialysis I had great difficulty concentrating on my work. As soon as I started with the treatments everything was much easier, my thinking was clearer.

In life there are always wonderful times, moments when you feel it was worthwhile being born. For me and my family such a moment occurred when I had my transplant, my "rebirth". After all those difficult years life at last seemed extraordinary. I didn't just live, I didn't just walk, I flew! I had to learn to live with the adverse effects of the medication but I was used to that since I had already done it a long time and I knew, as I mentioned before, that knowledge of what was happening was the key to my survival.

I must tell you of a funny thing that happened. One day as I was speaking rather loudly, in an aggressive tone, my daughter interfered and said, "Mom, is that you or the cortisone talking?" You see, it's important to understand the adverse effects of the medication and to analyze the impact on our life and our behaviour. My daughter had taught me a great lesson.

I believe that I am a very lucky person. I could not have fought this illness and had a full life and a full professional career without the love and help of those around me. In spite of his professional obligations, my husband always helped me, and after the loss of my health he took charge of the household. My husband and daughter were at my side, in good times and in adversity, and I thank them for it. Without them I would not be here, writing about all of this.

I retired two years ago, having been in public relations, a press agent and a communicator for part of my life. I have decided to devote myself to that which I love to do most—writing. Given my experience, I try to help young writers to become known. I belong to a creative writing workshop and I am a member of the board of directors of "La Société Littéraire de Laval".

It has been 16 years on December 4, 1996, since I had my kidney transplant. I carry this kidney as though it is my baby. It's a wonderful sort of pregnancy and I can only wish the same bliss to all those who are stricken with kidney disease.

68

Udo Canute, a 68-year-old man, began hemodialysis three years ago.

Dear fellow sufferers,

All of us have started off by seeing a doctor when we had kidney problems. Once in his office, we notice that various charts and medical drawings decorate his walls. "Is this the way I look inside?", we ask ourselves. While I myself had had many years of medical experience and had seen things like that before, to the newcomer a sober-looking doctor's office must be bewildering. The addition of a few scents characteristic of the profession, such as a whiff of rubbing alcohol, causes even the senses of the patient to become slightly confused. After this flustering first impression, an examination usually follows, with its numerous questions: when, why, where, how. Anyway, you all know what I mean. After this, the doctor recommends what should be done about the problem. You are given literature about catheters and dialysis machines, fistulas and what they do, the diet you have to follow, and the many other things that await you at the hospital. You check all the papers, make your next appointment and go home. By then, you are well on your way to becoming a hero.

You see, we have all gone through the next many steps of tests, x-rays and examinations that lead to being admitted to the dialysis unit. Indeed, a visit to the dialysis unit in action is a must for you. When you see the nurses running around with needles and trays or pushing drug waste-disposal baskets, when the blood flows through the many tubes on the machines, when pumps hum and dialysers are cleansing the patients' systems, you undoubtedly have the feeling that the people of the unit are exceptional human beings. Only determined people can withstand the many goings-on during their time on dialysis, which usually lasts between four and four and a half hours. The normal person would have already fainted at the idea of being a dialysis patient. However, these heroes, don't forget, are fighting for their lives; no dialysis for a few days (when one has no renal function), and life is at an end. The toxins will have quickly taken over. So these dialysis patients are a sturdy bunch. They help one another and they feel like a family. They feel with the other chum when things go wrong, such as when, unannounced, a needle pops out of a fistula. It is during these challenging times that the patient's resilience is truly tested: this makes heroes.

When I say that the people in the unit feel like a family, this includes the many partners of dialysis patients who are with their spouses during the long hours of dialysis. They not only comfort their partners but also help the other patients in many small ways. They transport them in wheelchairs, talk to the doctor and make appointments with them, constantly on the watch that everything is going well. At the end of a session, they are just as tired as the dialysis patient. The supporting husbands and wives who are doing their duties at home and in the office also deserve mention. Without their work, the dialysis patient could not survive. Actually, there is one heroine that I would like to mention specifically. She is the wife of a patient who was unfortunate to have lost both his legs to amputation. His brave wife is with him at any given time, picking him up in his wheelchair, getting him into the van, feeding him and the children and running a small business. This lady always has a smile, she always expresses hope and courage, and is an example for all to measure up to.

I have written this letter in order to help the people who have to climb this ladder, so to speak. Once dialysis becomes a matter of life and death, and a new patient enters the dialysis unit, he or she will soon become a "member of the club", fighting along with the rest of us to survive. Now, hopefully they can enter with a bit of inside knowledge that will make the transition a little easier for them.

69

Yves Noël, a 35-year-old man, began peritoneal dialysis one year ago.

Before I was diagnosed as having weak kidneys, I had noticed that my face, my feet and my fingers were swelling. When I went to the toilet I noticed that my urine flow was excessive. Sometimes I experienced fever, cold shivers and fatigue. These symptoms lasted for more than two months before I decided to consult a doctor to find out what was wrong. The doctor did blood tests and recommended that I start dialysis as quickly as possible because my kidneys had quit. I chose peritoneal dialysis because I could do it at home and therefore wouldn't have to come to the hospital three times a week.

Learning about my need for dialysis shocked me because I never believed that something of this nature could ever happen to me. I had been healthy and suddenly my kidneys didn't function anymore. I thought that this sort of thing only happened to old people. Also, the thought that I couldn't work anymore upset me. The doctor told me that such things could happen to anyone and then explained how dialysis works.

At the beginning of the dialysis I did my treatments four times a day. The treatments weren't easy because they were very tiring and I couldn't skip a treatment because the consequences were serious. My life changed completely because all my activities started to revolve around the dialysis. I couldn't visit with friends because I was always looking at my watch to see if it was time to return home for a treatment. I would have liked to do my treatments anywhere but I preferred to do them at home in a sterile room because I was worried about infection.

Before starting dialysis I couldn't keep my food down, I lost weight, I constantly felt tired and I believed I was going to die. However, after two to three months I noticed a great improvement in my health and I began to feel much better. Dialysis helped me considerably and more important, it saved my life. My wife helped enormously to overcome my shock. Luckily there were excellent doctors and skilled nurses, because if I had been elsewhere I don't know what might have happened to me.

Nowadays I try not to think about my dialysis. I try to read the newspapers and watch television. I take walks with my wife or by myself. I prefer to be alone because it helps me to meditate and reflect on my future, quite differently from last year when my morale was completely down because I constantly believed I was going to die. Even though those around me tried to comfort me, deep down I felt very depressed. The truth was hard but I had to accept it and go on living.

To those suffering from kidney failure I say you must accept things as they happen. You cannot do anything else. Count yourself lucky that there is a solution to your problem. There will be days when you will feel tired and discouraged but most of the time you will feel much better. Don't be upset too much because even in a normal life there are good and bad days. Don't think too much about the dialysis because that will weaken your morale and help to shorten your life. Try much harder to continue living your life as before and to see life positively because maybe someday there will be a miracle for your condition and everything will turn out for the best.

70

Robert Robillard, a 68-year-old man, began hemodialysis one year ago.

Before starting hemodialysis the nephrologist explained that I shouldn't be nervous about dialysis because there's nothing extraordinary about it. Before I started dialysis my health wasn't all that good. I blamed my condition on the lifestyle I had led. For example, at a certain time I smoked more than 60 cigarettes a day! In 1987 I had quintuple bypass to my heart. The doctor prescribed pills that were the equivalent of aspirin to dilute the blood and lessen the risk of blocking other veins. Unfortunately for me, those pills probably affected my kidneys. Dialysis has improved my health greatly, to the point where I haven't felt this well in 30 years. I feel so much stronger that I can even climb stairs now. I've never eaten this well in my life. I have a small problem with water because I can't have more than 33 ounces of liquid a day.

My wife looks after me and gives me lots of support. She's like a mother hen! I have found great comfort in playing bridge. Before I started on dialysis I owned my own bridge club and played five days a week, but with the onset of my illness I couldn't  look after the club so I sold it. Now I play bridge with friends three times a week so that, apart from my weekly bridge schedule which has changed, nothing else in my life has truly been affected by my dialysis treatments. On the contrary, thanks to dialysis my life has improved. I am also a member of an association of senior citizens who are on dialysis and I get great support from them. I intend to introduce them to the game of bridge and teach them how to play properly. I suppose my personality is also the source of strength. I also use humor in order to think positively.

For those of you who are about to start on dialysis because of weak or failed kidneys, don't be afraid, because for every problem there is a solution. I've played bridge for 63 years and I continue to play because I think of it as a therapy. Still I believe that everyone has a different form of therapy. As far as I'm concerned I would love to play bridge for the longest time possible. To realize this goal I will remain on dialysis, follow doctors' orders and stick to the rules of my diet. Consider yourselves lucky that you can have a solution to your problem because there are others who don't have this luxury and many who don't live very long after falling sick.

71

Mary Margaret Chamberlain, a 75-year-old woman, began hemodialysis a year and a half ago.

Before I started on dialysis, I had no pain and I did not feel anything different. The only thing that was a bit unusual was that I used to run to the washroom a lot. One day I got real sick and I went to the nephrologist who in turn sent me to the hospital emergency. I landed in the hospital

 with water in my lungs. The doctors found that I had three arteries in my heart that were blocked. While I was staying at the hospital I had a heart attack. The doctors at the hospital started me right away on dialysis in the cardiology department. Later I started coming to the hemodialysis clinic and I have been on dialysis since July of 1995.

When the doctor told me that I had to start on dialysis, there was nothing else I could do, and I just accepted it. There are a lot of surprises in this world and the best way to deal with them is to accept them as they come. I have been having a pretty decent life while I am on dialysis, and I would recommend it to anyone who is having kidney problems. Too bad they don't have a smaller hemodialysis machine, that way I could walk around with it and not lay down for four hours.

I have no family in Montréal, they are all living in different parts of Canada. I have been on my own for 52 years and that independence kind of helped me cope with dialysis. I have nobody to depend on anyways so I might as well depend on myself. I still have my own place and I still do the housecleaning and whatever I have to do around the house. I used to go bowling on Thursdays but I can't do that anymore because I have to get my dialysis. However I still go for little walks and play bridge at the church hall.

The only support that I received was from my sister, and that was when I first got out of the hospital. I was very weak at that time and I had no appetite. This past June all my three sisters came and stayed with me for about 10 days, so that was nice of them because their visit brought up my morale a bit.

There is one thing about dialysis and that is it makes me want to drink. However I am limited to only 40 ounces of liquids and that's pretty tough to control. I don't follow the food limitations too well but I try to stay away from ham, bananas, oranges and chocolate because the salt in the ham and the potassium in the fruit may hurt my heart. Sometimes I would like to go away on the weekends but I cannot do that because I have to come for dialysis on Saturday.

For those people who are about to embark on dialysis, the best way to deal with it is to accept it from the beginning, otherwise they'll be fighting all the way along. Just stop thinking about it. I haven't had any major problems since I am on dialysis and there is nothing to worry about. Dialysis ties you down a little bit but thanks to it you can live. Dialysis will never kill you, something else will. Some years ago people did not have a dialysis machine and they usually died. With a hemodialysis machine, you can hang on to your life.

72

Antonio Colabella, a 73-year-old man, began hemodialysis four years ago. His story is told by his wife, Mrs. Colabella.

Tony fell sick one year after his retirement. When he came to this hospital he was very sick and his kidneys were finished. Upon his doctor's advice, we threw out the medications that he was on because they were not good for his kidneys and for his diabetes. Before getting on dialysis, Tony could not walk or eat. I had to dress him, feed him, wash his face and bring him to the washroom. Many doctors examined him and gave him a lot of medication. Gradually, he began to walk, eat, and shave. For eight days we tried to do peritoneal dialysis at home but it was not good for Tony because his body was retaining water. The doctor operated to connect his blood supply to the dialysis machine several times. It did not work well for him in the neck, shoulder area or on the side of his stomach. Finally, making a fistula in his arm turned out to be successful. After a time, Tony's toe began hurting and it became black. This resulted from his diabetes. The doctor operated to remove it. Eventually, two toes from his other foot also had to be removed. He also had his appendix removed and he stayed in the hospital for three months. At that point he was so sick and did not eat anything for two months. I would ask him, "Tony, how are you? What's your name?" Slowly he began to recover with the help of medication and dialysis. Dialysis has been very good for Tony because now he can walk. If he had not gone on dialysis he may have died four years earlier.

When we discovered that Tony was sick we thought that he may die because he was too weak to do anything for himself. We have three sons and they were very happy that he was going to go on dialysis. Our eldest son encouraged Tony and told him that dialysis was going to be good for him. Many people encouraged him to go on dialysis telling him that it would make things better.

After being on dialysis for several hours, Tony is tired so he rests for a while and then has something to eat. He is diabetic so he stays away from salt and sugar. Every month or month and a half he has a piece of chocolate or some candy. He is doing so much better now that actually he is the one to remind me to do things. He sometimes goes outside and walks a little bit and when it is warm he enjoys sitting out on the terrasse.

Tony is the one with the courage to continue with dialysis and do things for himself. For example, when he experiences some pain and has to get up from the bed to go to the washroom, I tell him not to walk if it is going to hurt him but he finds the strength and the courage to continue doing things on his own.

Even if we have to come to the hospital for dialysis several times a week for several hours, it does not matter. All I care about is that my husband stays well. I am so happy with the care that Tony has received at the hospital. All the doctors and nurses have been wonderful.

73

Mr. Daoust (1923-1997) underwent peritoneal dialysis for three years. His story is told by his daughter, Jocelyne Bélair.

When my father learned that he had to start dialysis treatment, he had already retired and was surprised to receive the news. At the beginning it was very hard for him to accept, because it meant an enormous change in his life. Above all, my father had been an active person and this condition forced him to cancel some of his activities. This required a new adaptation for him, largely because of his age, but despite that, things have gone well with him, mostly because he has much support from his family and those around him.

Despite all the time that has gone by since he started on dialysis there are still times when he says, "If only I didn't have this...". That is why I believe that there should always be someone around to support him and lift his spirits. We always tell him that things aren't going as badly as he imagines and he often realizes that we are right. I believe it's important that those having dialysis should have someone always around for moral support. That's how we treat my father, telling him that things are going well, that he must continue and that he must never give up. I imagine that this is one of the secrets that will help him to overcome it.

Personally, I believe that when someone is in a situation where dialysis becomes necessary another important factor is strength of character. Somebody in such a plight is generally tempted to give up and indulge in self-pity. I suppose it's not easy to live with that, but in my father's case, he is someone with a strong character and so, when we visit him at the hospital and ask if all is well, he always seems resolved to pull out of it. He says it's because he has eight children, his grandchildren and his family. He also says that the people around him at the hospital are so fantastic that he can't let them down.

I also believe that when someone starts on dialysis it is very important for them to learn all they can about their medical care. I don't think they should live with unanswered questions, believing "maybe this, maybe that". Don't be shy to ask for help since questions about health are very important. Consult those who are aware and who can help, such as doctors and nurses. When you are uninformed you imagine all sorts of things that you are unsure of. I believe the best way to get rid of this is simply to ask questions.

What gives me strength and energy as a member of the family is that underneath everything one never knows what life can bring. One day I might also find myself in the same plight as my father, it can happen to anyone. Accordingly, if I can be of help to him, I'm very happy to be able to do it. We in the family have always been close to him, since when we were young he shared all of our experiences. Now, we feel it's important to us to live with what he is going through. I personally feel lucky that I have the chance of being so close to him and to look after him this afternoon.

74

Nellie Cecilia Brayne, a 77-year-old woman, began hemodialysis three weeks ago.

I'm having dialysis every second day. This will be my third or fourth treatment. After I get home I shall be on peritoneal dialysis. I'm supposed to come to the hospital three times a week for my treatments during which time I shall learn how to operate the peritoneal program. It takes far less time than coming to the hospital and I could look after it myself rather than be a millstone around other people's necks.

I came to the emergency because I was running off to the bathroom many more times that I should have. I was feeling tired and wanting to rest all the time which was very unusual for me. I was in the hospital for two weeks and then they sent me home putting me on pills because my bladder wasn't working properly. I saw the doctor and I was to come back January 30th, but I was in such a state that my niece recommended that I get in touch with emergency faster because you can't play around with this kind of trouble. When I discovered that I had to go on dialysis I felt a little bit of fear to begin with lest I were not able to do it. But at the same time I'm not ready to give up my life. I had the operation to install the catheter last Friday. I've had one flushing of it and the dressing was changed and I was told that everything was fine. I was scared to death before the operation but I'm a great believer in prayer. I felt I had a hand holding mine the whole time. The operation went very well. My doctor came to see me an hour or so after the operation. I was walking up and down the hall. She said, "You amaze me". I have been on the go all the time.

Our whole family support each other no matter what—good, bad or indifferent. We all mind our own business but we are there if any of us needs the other. I have a wonderful relationship with my family. That to me is very important. If you are a lone rock you feel timid but not if you have support of any kind especially true support like that of a family.

Now that I will be on dialysis I might have to cut back on some of the things that I do. Time will tell. I'm not going to be foolish and over-load myself but at the same time, an active mind is a healthy mind. You don't have time to feel sorry for yourself. Life is such that when you are affected by health problems, you have to pick up the pieces and carry on and not feel sorry for yourself. I feel my faith has made me whole. I feel it's my turn to repay all the help that has come to me by helping other people. I'm a great believer in being very active in the church. I have been in the church choir for 58 years and 64 years in the Altar Guild of which I am still a member. I'm very active in our Lakeshore Creative Stitchery Guild. I'm one of the editors of our newsletter. We have a jolly good time. Life is very pleasant. One lunch hour a week I go to Macdonald High School, which I attended, and I monitor the lunch hour in the computer room so that the children can use them. That is my job which I've been doing for four years. In our church I am secretary to the Parish Council. In our Senior's Club, I am responsible for sending get well cards, birthday cards, sympathy cards to those who are in need of them. I belong to the Christian Women's Club in Hudson in which we meet once a month and we have a luncheon and a speaker. I'm also on the telephone committee for that. I do a fair amount. I enjoy it. I feel that my outreach is to help somebody else.

Put your life in the hands of God. Many years ago I had a strange experience. I was in great stress over a problem which I had not brought on and nobody seemed to know why but I was going down, down, down in weight and reached a point where I could no longer cry. I had pains across my chest and down my left arm. My bed faced the window. This one night I said, "My God, please tell me whatever is wrong? How can I get rid of myself? I'm afraid of pain." I had a vision of Christ in his white garb with the flowing sleeves saying, "Suffer little children to come unto me". That vision came before me from the head down and the strong right arm came down, "You call yourself a Christian and you are thinking of this". "Take hold", and a second time, "Take hold." From that day on I never felt I was alone. I felt I had support with me all the way. That is what has been my stronghold. Really and truly, I feel God is there and He's offering help and all we have to do is accept and ask for it and the help is there. There's no greater help anywhere. I think every-body has a right to their own religion. There is only one God in my mind and we all have Him. This has befallen me and I must accept it and get on with the job. This hospital is a wonderful one. Every doctor, every person working for it do their best for every patient. We have to realize that they themselves are not gods. They're doing the best that they know, and we have to believe in them as we do in God.

75

Tara Robinson, a 26-year-old woman, began treatment nine years ago. Her treatments have consisted of peritoneal dialysis and two kidney transplants.

Finding out that I had a kidney problem and that I had to start dialysis was not easy, but my family provided me with a lot of support and really helped me get through it. This applies especially to my mother and my sisters, who are really supportive. In fact, my sister is considering donating one of her kidneys to me, so that I could have a transplant. My mother has already donated a kidney to me, and I had the transplant, but unfortunately the kidney failed. When that happened, I became really depressed, and I thought that I would be on dialysis forever. But now, I have regained my energy and my optimism through hoping. I think that I will not stay on dialysis forever, and that eventually I will have a successful transplant.

Although I receive much support from my family, my friends also provide me with important support in other ways. For example, I often talk to my male friends about some of the worries I have about being on dialysis. I wonder if a man would want to be with a woman who is on dialysis, and if he would, I wonder why. I have always seen dialysis as a burden, and I tend to think that it would also be a burden on another person. However, now I have developed a new attitude, and I do not really think that way anymore. I think that after all, dialysis is just something to get used to, and that there really is not much to it. In fact, I have one male friend who studies biochemistry, and is very accustomed to medically-related things. Because of that, he thinks that my being on dialysis is nothing at all. When people meet, they have to accept all types of things about each other, and according to him this is just another one of those things.

What I have to say to new patients is that things will not always remain as bad as they seem. At the beginning, starting dialysis seems hard, but it does get better. With time, it's possible to do many things, and I found that I was able to do a lot more than I expected. Before starting dialysis, I played a lot of sports, and I was actually able to continue doing this afterwards. The only exception was swimming, which I had to stop so I wouldn't get an infection. I'm also able to continue my studies, although it's taking me longer than it would have otherwise. I think that being on peritoneal dialysis allows me to have more time to do things, and that's one advantage of this type of dialysis.

There is one incident concerning dialysis which has remained very clear in my mind over the years. When I was at college a few years ago, I used to perform my dialysis treatments in the nurse's office during the day. One day, the nurse's husband found out that he had to begin dialysis. He was a teacher, and he was really worried about it. He thought he would never be able to go through with it. Then his wife told him about me, and she encouraged him that way. She told him that I was doing it, that it was possible, and that it was not that bad. I was really amazed when I heard that, and I thought it was quite incredible that my experience had served to inspire someone else. In a way, hearing about that gave me strength, and it increased my own energy and motivation.

76

A 64-year-old man (1932-1997) who wished to remain anonymous received hemodialysis treatment for two years following his heart transplant.

In June of 1991, I had a heart transplant. Ever since, I have been taking immunosuppressant drugs. These have had many effects on my body. They have affected my bones, caused kidney failure, and finally led me to develop lymphoma. The problem is that I have to keep taking these drugs, because otherwise my body might reject the new heart. It's a "Catch-22" situation.

Almost two years ago, I had to begin dialysis. Now I come to the hospital for dialysis and for all my other appointments. For me, it is impossible to believe that a hospital life can be a good life. But I do not have any other alternative. I think that I have had very bad luck until now. If people ask me whether I am better off with the heart transplant, I cannot answer them. That is because if I had not had the heart transplant, I would not be around today. Now, doctors want to build up my immune system so my body can fight the lymphoma. But they have to be careful not to build it up too high, or my body can reject the transplanted heart. Right now, I am walking a very fine line.

But I have to keep smiling. If I sit down 24 hours a day feeling sorry for myself, what kind of life will I have? I take things the way they are because I know that if I cry or yell, nothing will come out of it. In dialysis, I always feel dry and thirsty. Many times, I want to take a whole bottle of coca-cola and drink it down. It's not a pleasant life, but what other alternative do I have?

One thing I wanted very badly was to have a kidney transplant. But because I have lymphoma, this can never happen.

Nothing gives me support. I am sick physically, and not in my head. To me, it's not helpful to just talk and talk. I don't talk to the doctors, I diagnose with them. I ask them many questions. So far, the field of medicine is a very large field, in which many things have not been discovered yet. It's true that the field of surgery has advanced a lot. But there is one thing which I still require from it. When I had a severe heart attack, I received a heart transplant. Now my kidneys are failing, and I need a kidney transplant. How is this going to be possible?

Now, there are no known cures for AIDS or cancer. I know that I did not get cancer because of a genetic reason, but because of the medication I was taking. It's true that I rejected the heart transplant very severely, and that I had to take very high doses of immunosuppressants. Hopefully, when other people begin dialysis, they won't be coming into it with all the complications that I have.

If anyone with kidney failure thinks that they can survive without dialysis, they are being very foolish. For people whose kidneys aren't working, dialysis is a must. There is no such thing as maybe in a case like this. The only choice that people have concerning dialysis is whether to take it or leave it.

77

Frank Riccio, a 40-year-old man began treatment four years ago. His treatments have consisted of peritoneal dialysis and hemodialysis.

One day I went to a hospital and I was told I would need dialysis because I had kidney failure. They kept me there about two weeks, but I was not doing good. They weren't giving me the right medication and they did not have a dialysis unit like the one at this hospital. After two weeks I asked them if I could be moved. I called my brother and told him that I had to get out of that hospital. We contacted a doctor at the hospital and he told me that they did not have a place for me, but would keep me somewhere in emergency. It was snowing the night they rushed me over here. My brother came, my mother came too. I was left in emergency. The doctors came to see me and told me to relax and that everything would be taken care of. They said, "You are going to have dialysis and feel better." But I had never heard about dialysis, so I didn't know what it was. When I came in here I had 55 pounds of liquid in my body. For the first week they put me through dialysis and I felt better. I lost a lot of weight.

I am an accountant. I knew I was going to go through a lot of health problems, and my main concern was to find somebody that would take care of my business. So I found that person and she did pretty well. I was still concerned about my business. I came in March 1992 and income taxes are in March and April. She would give me a report every-day and tell me what was happening. So it was okay, and she succeeded in doing the income taxes, that was very important to me.

I had the choice of doing peritoneal or hemodialysis when I came out of the hospital. The fact of coming here three times a week I didn't like much, so I opted for peritoneal dialysis. It is the kind of dialysis you can do almost anywhere, but it has to be clean. I was doing peritoneal dialysis four times a day, three times at home and one time at the office. Everything was organized. I did this for one year, and I had to 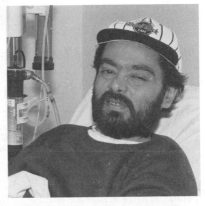 stop it because it was not working good for me.

Dialysis has prolonged my life. When I first came in here I saw all the tubes with blood and some people had them coming out of their arms and others from their neck, and I asked, "For me, where are you going to put the tubes?" They said that the first time it would be from my neck, and that scared me, but the doctors told me that they would freeze it and I wouldn't feel much. I had a lot of trust in the doctors that took care of me, even though I was told by doctors at another hospital that I had three hours to live, I still trusted the doctors here.

I can say now that that lady who today is my partner did a lot for me especially in the first month of my illness. My family did a lot too. I have one brother and two sisters. They helped me a lot too, they gave me a lot of support. I like to go out a lot, I like to go to the movies and I like to go to restaurants. My partner took care of this too, she brought me places to get the disease out of my mind, so that I can feel better. I can say that I had people around me that supported me a lot and because of these people, today I can say that I am on the transplant list. I can go through this thinking that everything is under control.

78

Jacques Piskopos, a 63-year-old man, began dialysis five years ago.

It was the summer of 1991 and I was in Greece and I was pretty good over there and then I came back from vacation and I went to see my daughter in California. Over there, my heart, it turned upside down and I started to not breathe. So my daughter, she took me to the hospital and they found that I had a lot of water. So they gave me an injection to make me pee and then they took me to emergency and they did a lot of tests. I had another attack of not breathing and the doctor said there was nothing they could do, we've got to put him on dialysis, so they put me on the machine. They connected me and they did dialysis and removed about eight pounds of water. After three days they took me again. They gave me two dialyses and then I said I want to go back to Canada. So they released me and I come here and I started dialysis here.

They explained to me that my kidneys, they went "kaput" and I needed dialysis. In the meantime I was sick. I don't know why, they didn't explain to me why. Nobody explained to me what is dialysis, what is going to happen, nothing. The only thing is I come here, I do dialysis and that's it.

I didn't have no reaction, nothing. I just come and have this done because I know that this is what my life depends on. If I decide to stay home I'm going to die in less than 15 days. So I don't want to die, I want to see my grandkids. I like to be free to come and go, to go to my daughter's to see her and my grandkids in California. Yes, I can do it but it is a big problem. Maybe one of these days when my leg is going to be okay I will go. My leg got hurt one Monday when I came to dialysis and I went to see my friend in self-care and there was water on the floor and I slipped and I broke my leg in six places. So maybe when it gets better. Otherwise everything is fine, everything is wonderful and I am glad there are these things that can make me stay alive.

It was the diabetes that caused the renal failure. I never watched myself. I ate sweets and everything, especially when I saw sweets it was crazy. I was like a little baby. In the beginning I was scared but I was a person who was sick all my life.

To a new patient, what can I say, this is the right decision, you do dialysis you going to stay alive, you don't you are going to die. I would say the same thing to a diabetic. I would say look at me, look how I am. Be very careful, watch what you eat, eat what you are supposed to, and no more than that, and stay away from sugar!

79

A man who wishes to remain anonymous began treatment 10 years ago. His treatments have been hemodialysis and a kidney transplant.

I'm a dialysis patient since 1986, it is nearly 10 years. Well, as a dialysis patient I have lots of problems—social problems, economic problems, materialistic problems. When I fell sick I had three children, and at that time they were very young. I never received help in my house, just myself. It is very tough, very hard, because after dialysis you feel very, very sick. You don't feel very encouraged. Then when I go for dialysis, afterwards I need to rest, 10 to 12 hours, and after that I feel strong, and I can do my housework, like cooking and cleaning.

One time I had a transplant, it did not last long. If it doesn't last long it is very painful, and I was very discouraged. At that time it was very painful, I don't know, maybe now the system has improved, maybe not. But I am waiting for another transplant now.

So far I am doing good. I walk a little bit, I socialize with friends, I invite them to my place or I go see them at their place. I also study at the library or read books, or I read Koran, or any books I find. That also helps me because I believe in Koran. So far in a materialistic way I live pretty normal, nothing changed, except I don't work now, and I am just hoping for a transplant, maybe then I can go back to work.

I did not have a lot of support when I started dialysis. I encouraged myself, my children helped me lots with their support. I come to the hospital for my dialysis treatment, and here it is pretty good with the doctors and nurses, most of them are really nice persons. They are efficient and very good, they give you moral support. I appreciate them, they do their job in a very nice way, if you have a problem they stand beside you.

When you are a sick person, it can never be normal, and when you are not working, it's very hard. You have to take it as it is, because you can't help it, it is not in your hands that you can change it. So when you have a medical problem, you have to keep this in mind, and you have to adjust to your medical situation. This is why I feel I have spent long enough in dialysis, and I am waiting for my transplant. Tomorrow I have an appointment to see a doctor about getting a transplant, I am looking forward to it.

For dialysis patients I have one piece of advice, make sure you clean your needling place with an iodine pad, it helps so that you do not get an infection in the fistula.

80

Kristine Shapiro, a 30-year-old woman, began treatment 12 years ago.
Her treatments have been peritoneal dialysis and two kidney transplants.

At the Hospital for Sick Children in Toronto we were told that my kidney function would continue to decrease slowly, perhaps one day necessitating dialysis. In 1977, when I was 11 years old, this was indeed a spectre that appeared more frightening than it would 10 years later when peritoneal dialysis was commonplace and kidney failure not a death sentence. Nevertheless, my kidneys kept me going (a miracle, to many) until the 12th grade when dialysis could no longer be forestalled, neither for faith healing, nor for fear; kidney function had dropped to almost zero. I wandered about my life in a zombie-like trance, poisoned physically and mentally from toxins my kidneys could no longer eliminate.

This was my transition into adulthood, ushered and carried by my parents who selflessly gave their attention, time and money to partner me through peritoneal dialysis training when I was too sick to learn alone. I remember my best friend later saying that the last two years of high school had been the best of that era for her; friendships deepened, boys began to notice, intellect arose and sharpened, ready to soak up every drop of nourishment available, and ready, too, to do battle with anyone, anytime. I can understand this now, for it happened this way for me too in a different place and a different time. But for that moment, time came to all but a stop. Literally freezing all the time, and in a walking stupor with no physical stamina and therefore no mental energy to socialize, I would drag myself to 8:00 am choir practice, then classes all day, at times holding my eyelids open so I wouldn't fall asleep. Exchanges were done in a handicapped washroom in spare moments.

As in my childhood, meanwhile, my parents prayed, as did their congregation, and many others, that I would be healed. I was then, and am now, grateful for their caring, although I used to get frustrated at being the subject of many a prayer-chain phone call and being known wherever I went as the "little girl with kidney problems". I suppose it was earlier than most, then, that I began my intellectual and spiritual journey on a path less traveled by adolescents, bypassing completely (by necessity) the pleasures of the flesh, and taking instead the cerebral road to maturity.

During my high-school years, I just tried to get through the moment, hanging on to short-term goals like good grades and winning the provincial French Speech competition. I spoke on the handicapped as we called "them" then, and generously peppered my speech with the various clichés I had heard so often and reviled. I took third place in that competition and somehow managed to come through high school with an A average. It never ever occurred to me to give up or to despair. This was not bravery. Bravery requires conscious choice, I believe, and therefore not to my credit, because intellectually I never struggled with this idea: to despair or not to despair. When people would constantly "compliment" me, saying, "How brave you are!", I would recoil, revolted. This was a stigma I did not want. I was not "the girl with kidney disease". I was Kristine who loved French classes and theatre and litera- ture and teddy bears. But my identity could not escape this brand: "the girl with kidney problems" (read: who may die) and who was (not) "brave", was thrust into a certain identity by virtue of her disobedient body which had come to rule her existence. I fumbled my way through high school and first-year university on dialysis in my hometown of Waterloo, forsaking friendships for study, until a kidney came one unex- pected day. This turned out not to be the blessing it seemed. It failed for technical reasons on the operating table (a clot formed in one of the main arteries which supply the kidney with blood, thus causing the new graft to starve), and complications snowballed until I was sicker than before. A month later I was out of the hospital and back on dialysis and back in school. Alright, I thought, too bad, I'll get another one soon. I'll just accomplish my education in the meantime. No big deal. I'm where I left off. Nothing gained, nothing lost. Who needs to party anyway?

The call for the second kidney transplant finally did come to eager ears on Christmas Eve as my family was heading off to bed after the traditional candlelight service in church. Visions of sugar plums danc- ing, yes, visions of transplant surgery, I had not envisioned! I was thrilled; it is like getting a personal telephone call from God herself (!) We really did jump up and down, excitedly blurting out the expected "What a wonderful Christmas present. A miracle! A new birth for me! etc..." This kidney indeed was my saviour of sorts: it was a successful transplant, and I blossomed forth like a new bud from a dry branch after a long winter. Upon opening my eyes after surgery, I mumbled, "I'm going to France now!" Dreams long forgotten and pushed to the back of my mind were now not only possible, but my body was going to allow me leave to accomplish them! Steroids boosted me sky-high: I could have been mistaken for a caffeine-junkie. Days after surgery, I was running up and down flights upon flights of hospital stairs. Nurses had to tell me to slow down. After years of hating food, I was now obsessed with it. I was cutting out tantalizing pictures and recipes from magazines the nuns brought around. I craved food every minute. I craved experience! I craved the life I had missed.

I was determined to do my part to get well again. I was bionic. I was invincible. I would chisel out for myself the life I wanted and the person I wanted to be. My level of desire for life's delicacies ran higher than my now normal hemoglobin. I loved existence.

And so I went to France. I finished my BA in English and French Literature, my MA in English Literature, and began my PhD. I moved out, made good friends, tentatively dated a little: I taught grade nine French part-time and first-year university essay writing, moved to Montréal, and, best of all, there unexpectedly met my husband, Theodore Shapiro, a fellow-Virginian (I was born and adopted there) studying in Vermont. We married in July 1994 and moved to Mississippi where I could continue my lone research for my Doctorate in English while Ted did his Master's in Meteorology. Life was looking good. Perhaps, I thought, I might even live beyond 30, after all (in fact, I had always found it hard to imagine myself as an adult) and, could it be true, really be a normal person, a wife, a professor, and even, one day, a mother?

But May 1995 brought other plans. After celebrating Mother's Day in Ontario with my family and my grandparents, Ted and I proceeded to visit Montréal (where my supervisor was, and where there was the culture we were starved of in Mississippi) on what we thought was one stop on our way home. I never left. After five days of nausea to the point of fainting, headaches, and general malaise in a Montreal hotel room,

I lost my 10-year-old kidney. When Ted and I heard the diagnosis, the skies came crashing down around us. We held each other and cried on my hospital bed. I felt in one moment the loss of everything I held dear. And yet, we both had never felt closer to each other than in this moment of pain.

But this time, unlike before, it did occur to me to give up, and to despair. The struggle is much harder now, being no longer innocent of suffering and its ends, which are not always rewards. I was aware, bitterly, of how bad things can happen over and over to good people for no reason at all, while others flit through life, successful and unscathed. I had my husband to consider now, not to mention my hoped-for career; my very future as a live human being was at stake. I resolutely refused to play games of silly optimism and cheery blindness to reality. I felt physically the loss of any former notion of grace and hope. I felt, too, the loss of a normal marriage, and of my sense of femininity (so hard-won) as images of catheters and more scars and a pregnant-size tummy filled my head. I saw my real hopes of teaching university literature flee along with travel; even life itself, for the first time, seemed to be making a quick exit out the door. Despair and anger settles like a black cloud. Still, I had to buoy up my husband, to keep him from losing sight of a possible future, a healthy one, together. He would not, I would not allow it, be a "caregiver" as if he was 85 and I was ill, forever. His presence forced me to fake optimism. And sometimes that is enough to stay afloat physically, and to plant a real seed of optimism, although one is imbued heavily with knowing paradox and shadow, in one's own mind.

A year and a half later, Ted and I survive. We survive, and we fight to keep surviving, physically and emotionally, because it is our only option. We want to share a future and all its possibilities. We have had many many moments, understand, where all the philosophies of love and hope and survival seem weak-kneed and impotent, mere castles built in the air to live in for the moment. We feel claustrophobic; my illness invades every waking and sleeping moment. Conversations center around continual crises, not the seeming frivolous plans of our peers. At times, we resent them. We are sometimes angry that life has done this to me again. Haven't I suffered enough? There is no sermon or homily to be gleaned here. But, somehow, miraculously, hope remains. I fall, and the rebound is joyous in comparison. I believe in the future, and therefore in life, still. I can still read and take joy in it. That in itself is enough to slug it out with fate. Despite the daily routine of dialysis, I can see beyond this vale to a future filled with purpose and meaning, laughter and joy.

81

Bruce Kinsella, a 66-year-old man, began hemodialysis six years ago.

I have a disease called polycystic kidneys, a slow progressive affliction. I learned of this problem around the age of 40 through one of my sons who was seven years old at the time. He passed blood in his urine one day and we panicked. We rushed him to the hospital, where they kept him under observation for two weeks, before releasing him. When they released him he didn't seem sick and his urine cleared up, but his doctor had a suspicion it was polycystic kidneys. As a result he asked the whole family to come in for tests. As it turned out, all five children are afflicted, plus myself.

I was put on blood pressure medication and lived quite a normal life until I approached the age of 60, when I was informed I would soon have to go on dialysis, as my kidney function dropped to about 17 percent. They arranged the operation for a fistula. I thought this would be very painful, but it wasn't that bad. The surgeon froze my arm by inserting a needle in my neck and pumping fluid in, which completely paralyzed my arm. Therefore, I felt nothing, and there wasn't much pain after. I really feared this operation at first because I never had one before in my life.

Well, I've been on dialysis for six years now and have had many operations since. One very serious operation was a quadruple heart bypass, which turned out to be a complete success, although the recovery time was a good four months. I feel that the heart problem was caused by dialysis. Other operations that I had were for new fistulas. The first fistula lasted about four years, then I had a couple more operations on my left arm, which eventually failed. When a fistula fails, they have to put a catheter in your chest or your groin so you can continue to be dialyzed until a new fistula can be installed. Just recently I had a new fistula in my upper right arm, which has developed very well and I am now needling again. They have also removed the catheter from my chest.

Shortly after I went on dialysis I stopped working. One of my major concerns was, how was I going to get money. The company that I had worked for offered me my pension in a lump sum, or so much a month, I took the lump sum and put it in a locked RRSP. At that time the interest rate was pretty high, and in two years I think I increased my pension by $20,000. But still, I needed money. I was able to get the Provincial Disability Pension, which was pretty good, then I decided to transfer my RRSP to an annuity, and started collecting on that. My father had died and my aunt had died, and they had both left me money, that helped. Then when I turned 65 I applied for a Federal Pension. So with the

three of them I manage. That's a big concern. I remember when a new patient came in here, his wife came and sat beside me, and asked all types of financial questions. She was very worried, her husband lost his job, and she didn't have a job. So I told her what I used to do, I helped her quite a bit.

I just accepted dialysis, I didn't worry about it. I have been thinking about getting a transplant lately. I inquired about it but I am not on the list yet, I don't know whether I will go through with it or not. I feel better now that I am on dialysis, it doesn't frighten me.

There's a lot of things I can't do now. This year with all the operations that I had, I was unable to play golf... maybe next year, and I couldn't travel, with the problems I was having with the catheter, I am afraid to travel. I used to go to P.E.I every year, my wife is from there. Well, if this keeps working well, maybe next year I can go.

My wife and children are very helpful. My wife is wonderful. For a while I couldn't even change, I couldn't dress, I couldn't bathe, and she was a wonderful help. When I was in the hospital, for my bypass, my children and my wife came every day. This support makes life a lot more pleasant.

82

Elaine Ashton, a 51-year-old woman, began treatment five years ago. Her treatments have been peritoneal dialysis and two kidney transplants.

I was diagnosed with glomerulonephritis in October of 1986. This is an autoimmune condition whereby the immune system gets turned on but refuses to turn off. My kidneys were not recognized as "mine" so were attacked. At that point, approximately 40 percent of my kidney function had been destroyed. The only hope to stop the damage was massive doses of cortisone to heal the kidney and immunosuppressants to stop the activity. Even if this treatment worked, the prognosis of the condition indicated that recurrence of the condition was almost inevitable and dialysis eventual in a 10-year time frame.

This news was a complete shock to me since I had always been blessed with good health. Unfortunately that had all changed on New Year's of that year (coincidentally my 41st birthday). That was the day I was admitted to the hospital emergency department. I had been suffering for a week with what I thought was a bad case of the flu. The actual cause turned out to be a massive ovarian cyst. The surgery to remove the cyst included a complete hysterectomy. Although cancer had been a strong possibility and my family prepared for the worst, this, fortunately, was not the case. The "flu" of the previous week involved all the basic flu symptoms. I had a raging fever for days which went untreated. It was the holiday period and my daughter was away most of the time. My mother and sister checked in with me daily by phone but I was largely by myself burning away. Since high sustained fevers do impact on the immune system, I trace my eventual kidney problems to this incident.

The massive cortisone treatments were medically successful but the side effects of the drug made for a "year from hell". Two years later, I received the dreaded news that the condition had reactivated. I went home, curled in a pre-natal position and cried for the first time because I knew, no matter what happened after this point, I would never be "normal" again.

I am very fortunate to have a close and loving family all of whom share a keen sense of humor (our Celtic roots) and an overall optimistic attitude about life. These are things that money can't buy.

As the years progressed my condition was closely monitored and I had regular check-ups at the hospital. Many of the patients I have talked to were suddenly confronted with the fact their kidneys had failed and the reality of dialysis thrust upon them whereas the gradual decline I experienced was, I'm sure, easier to experience.

As my kidney function decreased so did my energy level. My sleep was constantly disturbed by violent leg cramps and annoying, persistent itching. There came a point where dialysis started to look "attractive" and I started asking serious questions about the two methods available. I have found it interesting how dialysis patients decide on the choice of method (hemo or peritoneal) depending on their personalities and situations. When I was told about the fistula and needles involved in hemodialysis I must confess my personal conceits and keen dislike of needles made my choice of peritoneal dialysis inevitable. The idea of having to trek up to the hospital three times a week in winter weather was the absolute selling point.

The following is a list of comments on my experience with CAPD:

- Once I started dialysis I quickly felt better. The frequent feelings of nausea and leg cramps were no longer a problem.

- The staff at the CAPD clinic are truly supportive and have a wealth of experience with other patients from which to draw. It's important to tell them if you have any problems.

■ One needs a fair bit of space to store the dialysis liquids which are delivered monthly.

■ For the first three years I was on dialysis, I "only" needed to dialyze three times a day. This sounds pretty awesome but one quickly adapts and it becomes second nature. The process takes about 25 minutes but I used the time to do other things in my normal schedule. In the morning I did my hair and makeup, after work I read the paper and before going to bed I watched the news while I was dialyzing.

■ When it became necessary to do a fourth daily dialysis, it did present problems since I was working full time. I was supplied with a cycler that allowed me to hook up to the machine overnight while a series of automatic exchanges are performed throughout the night. Since peritoneal dialysis is painless, sleeping was never a serious problem. This method left my days free.

■ The company which delivers the dialysis liquid will arrange to have material delivered to places where you travel. I travel frequently to Vancouver but have also had deliveries to a remote country inn near Sherbrooke and my country home in the Laurentians. CAPD offers more flexibility than hemodialysis where one needs to be relatively close to a hospital for dialysis three times a week. Off the beaten track trips must be a serious challenge when one is using the hemo method.

I worked full time until two years ago but was really feeling weary. One day, on a whim, I inquired at our personnel department as to the eligibility requirements for the long-term disability leave. To my amazement, they sent me home that very day on instant retirement! I must admit I've appreciated the release.

In November 1995 I received a call that a kidney had been found for me. Several days after the operation it was obvious there was a problem. Unfortunately the donor kidney had a flaw in the artery which prevented adequate blood to the organ. Ten days after the first operation I had another to remove the kidney. All that misery for nothing!

On January 29, 1997, another compatible kidney was available. This time the operation was a success. The week after the transplant, I experienced persistent low-grade fevers. After the previous transplant it was an anxious time but the problem was rectified by actually reducing the drug dosages. Since that time I am experiencing a metamorphosis! My renewed energy is amazing. For the first time in a long time I can allow myself to think about tomorrow. I have a life again!

83

Zopito Mariotti, a 70-year-old man, has been undergoing hemodialysis for three years.

I began feeling very sick and I was vomiting all the time. The doctor operated immediately and removed one of my kidneys. It has been three years since I am on hemodialysis. Now I eat normally and I drink but I have to be very careful about how much I drink. So many times I drink too much and I am obliged to go to the emergency during the night. At the emergency they give me oxygen and later I go for kidney dialysis. I have been to the emergency about 15 times. I drink too much and I feel that I cannot breathe. I never again want to reach this point. My wife has lost some courage because of this. It is important that I drink less so I have learned how to adjust my drinking.

When I arrive home after having been on dialysis for four hours I feel very tired. I eat something and then I go to sleep at eight o'clock. The next day I feel good because I have rested and slept. I feel no pain and I eat and drink all that my wife gives me. She makes sure, however, not to give me such things as oranges, chocolate, and bananas. I have a lot of medication to take. I have requested a kidney transplant and I am now waiting for a kidney which I think will take two years. I want to help other people and the advice I would give to new patients is to not be scared.

The doctor asked what inspired me to request a kidney transplant. I told him that I was almost 70 years old and I do not want to die. I still go out dancing with my wife. I get support from my wife, family and friends. I have a son and a daughter who are both married but when I need something they come right away and this makes me very happy. I have one grandson and two granddaughters who are aged five, eight and 12. My five-year-old granddaughter knows which days I am in the hospital. She asks her mother if she can call "Nono" and then when she comes to see me, she kisses and hugs me and asks how I am feeling. When I was in Italy my granddaughter even called me from Montréal to ask how I was doing. My family and friends in Italy and in Montréal were very happy when they heard that I had requested a kidney transplant. Since being on dialysis I have made new Italian friends who are also on hemodialysis and we enjoy talking and laughing together.

84

Giovanni Vigorito, a 50-year-old man, began treatment 22 years ago. His treatments have been hemodialysis and two kidney transplants.

My kidney failure started in 1974 and was caused by high blood pressure. The first treatment I received was hemodialysis. The doctors put my name on the list for a kidney transplant, and 14 months later my turn came. My kidney transplant lasted for about 16 years but unfortunately, the transplanted kidney became tumorous and I had to go back to hemodialysis for another four years. Luckily, I was given another chance for a kidney transplant which I received in May of 1996.

I was 28 when I was diagnosed with kidney failure. The news did not affect me much because I always had courage to deal with anything. It's been more than 20 years now that I am having treatment for my kidney and I still have more courage to deal with whatever is awaiting me.

There was a big difference between hemodialysis and kidney transplant. With the latter I could live a normal life. I could go anywhere anytime I wanted to. When I was on the hemodialysis machine, I could not go away because I had to be on it three times a week. With a kidney transplant, I could eat anything I wanted, and there was no limitation on the amount of liquids I could have. I still have to watch my salt level but that does not bother me. Today, I look so healthy that people don't think I have a kidney transplant. Having a kidney transplant made a big difference in my life because it gave me more energy which enabled me to have two kids.

Sixteen years after my first transplant, my doctor told me that I had to go back on dialysis because the transplanted kidney was tumorous. I refused to go back on dialysis because I was still feeling very well and I ran away from the hospital. I made my doctor wait for 14 months before I finally agreed to remove the kidney because the tumor was getting bigger and I started to feel tired. That was not my first time on hemodialysis and the transition went smoothly. When the doctors found out that the tumor belonged to the donor, I was eligible to put my name on the waiting list for a kidney transplant again. I always told my doctor whenever I saw him that I could not wait to get a kidney and urged him not to forget about me. Week by week, month by month, year by year my turn came and I had my second transplant.

I have a good relationship with my family. My wife encouraged me and supported me throughout my sickness. At first she used to come

with me to the hospital. Later she realized that there was no need for her to accompany me to the hospital because I had no problem driving myself to do my dialysis. I am happy with my kids. I take them to school and I play with them in the park. My two kids give me the power to live.

I know that I have a kidney transplant and that I am taking medication but I don't think about my sickness. I am happy all the time and

I keep the sickness to myself. All I have to do is to just turn my head around to see people who need more help than me and I thank God that I am in better shape. Some people are sick because they don't stop from thinking about their ailments. They stay at home all day and that's not good for their psyche. They should go and talk to other people. I live my life day by day until it's over. I don't worry about what's going to happen tomorrow. Tomorrow is another day and life goes on.

85

An 80-year-old woman who wishes to remain anonymous began hemodialysis three years ago.

I had a heart attack, I thought it was angina, but all the time it was a heart attack. I had a blockage, and for the blockage they had to inject some kind of an ink dye, but this ink dye would affect my kidney function. The doctor talked to me very carefully, and told me that if I didn't have the ink dye injected I would probably have another heart attack and die. So I had a choice, to live on dialysis, or not have dialysis and die. They injected me with the ink dye to tell them where the heart blockage was, and that finished my kidneys, like they told me it would. So that's how they put me on dialysis. That was three years ago and I've been fine.

At the beginning it was difficult, I didn't know anything about it, but the more I'm on, the better I feel. I'm not scared or anything like that. I knew what it was in a way, because my sister was on dialysis. If we didn't have dialysis, where would we be? At first it's hard, I didn't know what it was like to have the needle in your arm, but they find a way. The nurses freeze my arm and I don't feel nothing. If they didn't freeze me, I wouldn't be able to take it. Some people prefer to do the dialysis themselves, but I would rather come to the hospital and have the machine and the doctors there, because they know what they are doing.

This is my kidney machine, I don't know how to say it better, if I didn't have that, I wouldn't be. Dialysis didn't change my social life too much. I can go swimming if I want and if I'm able, I can ski, and I can do anything. Sometimes I think I can do things much better now, because before I was tired. As a matter of fact, since I started dialysis I go out more. If I didn't have to come to the hospital, I probably would stay at home more. These people are very good to me, they are like my friends. It's a routine now, so there's nothing to be worried about or scared about. The science is advanced, maybe in the olden days people used to die from kidney disease, but they have things for us to save our lives now. Now, old or young, they can save you. We are lucky to have this.

I got stuck at the hospital once in a snowstorm. I had to go to emergency after my dialysis, and I asked the guy, "What am I going to do?" He said to me, "What do you think this is, a motel?" I said, "I beg your pardon, but this is emergency, and when you can't go home and you are stranded, don't you call that an emergency?" So, I came back to the dialysis unit, but it closes at night, and the nurses sent me to a room upstairs in the hospital. It was cold in the room, and they brought me a blanket, but I didn't sleep because it was too cold. I was anxious to go home when the storm was over. One woman came up to the room to see me and brought me a coffee. I said, "Do I look frozen?" and she said, "Well, you don't look too comfortable." I went downstairs to the dialysis unit before I left and saw one of the nurses. She asked me where I had slept, and I said, "I am wondering if it was not the place where they keep the corpses." That was it, it was a little adventure, I thought it was funny. I was so happy to get home. That day I didn't have to do dialysis, and I'll tell you, when I got home I went straight to bed and I slept.

86

Kenneth Mah, a 29-year-old man, began treatment nine and a half years ago. His treatments have been hemodialysis and a kidney transplant.

When I discovered that I needed to go on dialysis in 1987, I didn't like the idea, and in fact I was very much afraid of the idea even though I had been expecting it for a while. I think the worse thing was the needling part. These things are huge. When you first take a look at them you're thinking, "these are going in me?! I think not!" It requires surgery on top of that to prepare the fistula. I started to think about the fact that my arm would become quite scarred. There was the cosmetic aspect such as how am I going to explain this to people if they see? I still wondered how I was going to pull this off, like how I was going to go to school and come to the hospital at the same time. One of my prime concerns was how I was going to keep this from people. I didn't want it to intrude in my normal life. I think I was actually quite successful keeping it from people. No one knew until I actually got a transplant. In fact, I didn't even tell my dad when I first started. I didn't want to worry him with this because I knew that he would make a big deal out of it. I pulled that off for a couple of sessions and then he finally insisted on accompanying me to where I was getting my "treatment", which he thought would be temporary. That was actually quite funny. It carried a huge stigma so I didn't want my parents to see that.

I was ecstatic when I learned I was going to have the kidney transplant. It was my ticket out of dialysis. After three and a half years I finally got it. My doctor had warned me that it might be complicated in my case because I have a host of other medical problems. I went ahead with it anyways. I don't think I consciously acknowledged the problems that could happen. I expected that things would be perfect afterwards. After the transplant, life was better in terms of freedom, but the kidney was quite problematic from the beginning, especially the first six months or so at which point I was in and out of the hospital. It was devastating when the kidney failed three and a half years ago. Looking back, it was very interesting to see how much I was in denial because I thought that the doctors were wrong and if I just took more medications it would clear up.

I went through a fairly deep depression. It was just time that brought me out of it. I was not happy even when the depression ran its course. I certainly wasn't happy coming back to the hospital. I totally dreaded it. After a while, I went through another depression about being back on dialysis. I think it was an even more severe depression. I don't know if there has been a lot of positive movement. I've just been told that I will probably go back on the transplant list very soon because they did some tests and things are apparently good or at least adequate. If you would have asked me about getting a transplant when I had my first one, I would have said yes despite all the problems. Now I would say that I'm not so sure after having gone through the rejection and the pain which was very devastating. I have a lot of questions and concerns that I would like to take up with the transplant doctor. I think that there is a lot of sense of hopelessness. Why bother? Why should I go through that if it's just going to be problem after problem? I could look at my quality of life in absolute terms or in relative terms. Absolutely, it's not bad although there are problems that keep cropping up, especially in my case with all these other attendant problems. Relatively speaking, if I compare myself to my peers at school, I keep envying them. They can take their lives for granted; I can't. They can go traveling whenever they want; I can't. They don't have to worry about dietary concerns; I have to. They don't have to come to the hospital three times a week and lose five, six hours per session of their life here. There's a lot of envy. There's always been. I find that it's getting harder to pull off trying to be as "normal" as possible in a "normal" world because I've seen enough doctors and nurses and hospitals for 100 people. It batters at you. You have to be part of the system. You either come here and subject yourself to all this or you die. I have to say I'm not afraid of death. I guess it's that sense of hopelessness creeping in. The future does not look very pleasant.

People have told me that they have been impressed by my determination to get my PhD. I feel like telling them to please not congratulate me on something like that. It's still like trying to lead that "normal" life but sometimes it creeps in on me that this is a facade. I like my academic life but I wish I could appreciate it without having these problems on my mind. Whatever sense of normality it gives me and whatever sense of anticipation for the future, it's always clashing against my hospital life or my role as a patient, if you want to put it that way. My role as a patient has affected my self-esteem and self-image. You get subtle reminders when people in your "normal" life say, "How are you?", in that sympathetic tone. Ever since I've come to Montréal, I've been a lot more open. People seem to be very accepting which is very nice. It is a comfort and it takes away from the stigma. If I've gone through a particularly rough period and I feel like venting, there's always someone who will listen to me, but I don't think I do that too much. I'm still a very private person. I am almost intensely private which surprises me to see myself doing this interview, but it's for a good cause.

Socially, I don't think dialysis has hindered me too much unless you count the times I've been in the hospital instead of elsewhere. Before I started dialysis for the first time and found out that my kidneys were failing, I became absolutely fanatical about following dietary restrictions. Once I actually started dialysis, it was like a 180° turn where I went back to my normal habits. If I went out with friends to eat, in my mind I thought that if I requested no salt or asked them to limit the amount of beverage that I could take in, it would have seemed strange to people and they would have started asking questions. I was quite the bad little patient in Winnipeg. The dietitian and the doctor would ask me, "Have you been eating Big Macs again?", and I of course would say, "No", and we'd all laugh.

I very much resent being called a hero. For people who have not gone through an experience like this, it seems like there is a need to idealize things or to put things on a pedestal to encourage people to keep their chin up.

It's as though they're telling them to cope in an ideal way, according to their expectations. This is related to my earlier statement about how people are impressed with how I try to maintain a normal life while going through all of this. Please don't congratulate me on something like that because I don't want to hear it. People think it's some sort of super-human effort to try to maintain a normal life, but it's not. Putting an idealistic spin on something like this seems like propaganda. Do you really know what people are going through? What is your concept of a hero? I would very much like to know because it doesn't jive with my concept of a hero at least in my case. It doesn't quite encompass the range of coping styles. Clearly, there are negative sides and I'm sure most, if not everyone, goes through negative periods and not all of them come out unscathed. If the aim is to encourage future patients, leave my story out and just put in all the happy little stories, but I think that does a great disservice to future patients. Some patients are going to think that it may not be so bad, and for some of them it may not be so bad, but other people are going to be unpleasantly surprised. There is a whole range of ways in which people can cope.

87

Léo Tavormina, a 34-year-old man, began hemodialysis one year ago.

My story is one without any history, it just happened. One morning I got up and I was bloated and everything. The night before I had just played two games of football so I was healthy and running and everything. Before that I had some general fatigue but I chalked that up to some kind of a flu and then I had some stomach upset but no pains, but I chalked that up too because I had never been sick a day in my life. I stay in pretty good shape so I could never really comprehend anything like this happening, especially when it isn't in the family. It hasn't existed in the immediate family nor in the extended family, nobody had any kind of disease like this. I didn't even know what kidney disease was.

I remember, I just woke up and I was bloated and I couldn't breathe and my feet didn't fit in my shoes. We were actually in Toronto for a football tournament so my teammates said "Oh, you probably ate something last night, the restaurants here are not that good!" So I actually dressed for the game because I figured if I ran a lap maybe it would be okay. So I started running and I just didn't have the energy. I just couldn't breathe so I decided I would sit out and watch that game. The next day was the last game so I said that I would watch the last game rather than go to a hospital in Toronto, just in case I had to stay a while, I would drive back and just go check in over here because at least I would be in Montréal. I have a wife and kids and I didn't want there to be trouble. So we drove back and I came here and that was actually Thanksgiving last year. Just from the symptoms they kind of suspected it but they did some tests and the tests confirmed it—so that was a shocker.

Naturally I started off in some sort of denial saying that it must be some kind of infection. But I was here in the hospital for about five or six weeks. They couldn't believe that I was actually playing the night before because according to them my levels like my potassium and everything else were so high that they couldn't even believe that I was able to walk. They were saying that I should have been dead a long time ago.

They couldn't get the levels down in one dialysis session because they were amazingly high according to them. So they had to do it over a couple of weeks. Meanwhile over those couple of weeks I was really getting worse as far as fatigue and energy. I wasn't feeling sick as far as mentally out of it or any pain. After about two weeks they let me go home for the weekend. Where I live there are four steps and I couldn't even make it up four steps, for me that was unbelievable.

Meanwhile while I was in the hospital I learned a lot about what I had. The street term is Berger's disease and the medical term is IgA. And I learned that there are no real symptoms or signs and 99.9 percent of the time it is benign but once in a while it hits somebody and seizes the kidneys. After about the first two weeks of being in the hospital, after being down and out and really crying and the works I pulled myself up again and I convinced myself that if I was going to have to live with it, I was going to make the best of it. That's when my spirits started picking up again and by the time I was discharged from the hospital my spirits were up. I said if I have this, I'll just do the dialysis. Meanwhile I chose hemodialysis. The reason I chose that was because of my lifestyle. I still loved to run. I still wanted to play football and if I would have any other system I wouldn't be able to do that.

Hemodialysis takes up about a total of 15 hours of your time a week for the rest of your life. The rest of your life could be good if you make it good so that's what I told myself. I said I was going to make it good so I started running. I made it back up by January. This happened in October and by January I was back up to about 45 minutes a day again. The doctors said to take it easy but I said I know my body, I know if I am pushing it too much.

At that time I had one daughter and I have my second one now. We were planning for a second or third child and when they told me that kidney disease affects your fertility, I said, "Oh no that's terrible." I was more worried about that than anything else. And we had a second child after I started dialysis so I was like, all right! Without my wife and kid, I don't know if I would have made it through. They were my emotional support, my spiritual support and they were there beside me a 100 percent.

I tell people, when they ask me how I feel, that if I didn't have to show up for dialysis three times a week I would never know that I was sick. There are two things that remind me that I am sick , coming here and when I feel my fistula. Dialysis is doing what it has to do and I am doing the rest with my body. I'm eating well, I am watching my diet, I am staying fit, I do light training with weights and I do a lot of running. The first thing I did when I got out of the hospital, because our football season starts in April, was I made a brace for my arm and I went right off to training camp. I played and we just finished our season last week. The only thing that has changed is that I can't drink as much but that is the limit. I do everything that I was doing before. I work, I do everything.

The nurses and the doctors here are great, they do everything I ask of them and I do the rest. I'd say to look into yourself for answers and make things work for yourself. Don't necessarily depend on the medical field to give you all the answers. If you look into yourself and then push your body, your body will respond. That is my philosophy, not in a religious sort of way but in a self-confident, positive attitude way, in that sense. You make things happen. And I wasn't supposed to go running two months later but I knew that I could or at least I thought I could and I proved myself right. So now I start dialysis at 7:30 a.m. I bike in around 5:30 a.m. and I go for a run on the mountain and then sit down—that's how I fit everything into my schedule.

I don't consider myself a hero. I'm just proud of myself in the sense that I don't let things stop me. I would probably do it anyway, as an individual, because it's just in my character but my courage to go on is for my family. I mean my little daughters make everything all worth it.

88

Annette Spunt, a 73-year-old woman, began hemodialysis five months ago.

I didn't know I had kidney disease. I was going to the doctor and he was taking blood tests and that's when he discovered it. Needless to say I was devastated, but just gradually, I sort of got used to the idea. I had an idea of what dialysis was because my daughter-in-law's mother was on it. I didn't know how to do dialysis, but I had a good idea of what it was all about. I have to come here three times a week, so it has changed my life. I don't work, but I have a husband who has had two strokes, so I have to be caring for him a bit. It's not easy.

I don't cope with the specialized diet too well. I used to drink six to eight glasses of cold water a day, now I find it very difficult to cut down on the liquids. I had to cut out a lot of foods that I liked. I used to like chewing on a carrot or a piece of celery, but I can't continue doing that. It's not easy, and sometimes I cheat. I am not allowed bananas, but I love bananas so they allow me a banana in the morning. After breakfast I have one just before I go on dialysis, otherwise I can't eat them. I am also a diabetic, so I have to keep away from sweets. Since I'm on dialysis I have put weight on, my appetite has increased. I have to start watching my weight again.

Every year we have been going to Florida for two months of the year. Seeing that I am on dialysis I am not too anxious to go. The doctor has told me that there are a lot of places to do the dialysis and there's no problem with that, but my husband does not seem to want to go. To go and fly around, it's not easy for him either. We're going to have to be locked in the house this winter.

My family has supported me, they do what is possible, but they have their own lives, I can't expect too much. My children keep telling me that things could be much worse: "Dialysis is not the worst thing that could happen to you." So I sort of take it in stride.

I spoke to the doctors about a transplant, but I had a heart operation five years ago, and he said that it was not a good idea.

My husband and I are home most of the time. We go out during the day when we can, when the weather is good, but not much on the social side. I did join a social group for people my age at the shopping center. We have meetings every Wednesday. I try to get there and get out of the house to see people and talk.

The advice I would give people that are entering dialysis is, don't be petrified. The first time you come in it's pretty scary. You come sit down and they put the needles in, you get a little frightened, but then you sort of get used to the idea. It's not perfect, but it's something you have to live with, and it's either that or death. I don't want to die yet, I have grandchildren and I want to enjoy them.

89

Mr. Nguyen, a 68-year-old man, began hemodialysis four years ago.

One day I went to see a doctor and after having a blood test he told me it was time for me to start dialysis. When my doctor said that to me I thought that I would have to have dialysis treatments two or three times only and that afterwards I wouldn't have any problems. I was really surprised that I would have to do it for the rest of my life. At first, when I learned that my kidneys were at the terminal stage, I also believed that everything had come to an end for me as well. I thought I was finished. I had another surprise when I started on dialysis and realized that I felt much better than before, and that dialysis would help me to live much longer.

I came to Canada 21 years ago from Vietnam, my place of birth. In my country I was in business, but when I came here I only found work as a security guard. Since Vietnam was a French colony, I spoke French before coming here. I also learned English during the Second World War and I also speak Chinese and of course, Vietnamese. I could also speak Japanese at one time, but I have forgotten it all now. Presently I am in retirement and I live alone, therefore my dialysis doesn't affect my schedule. As well, I live separately from my wife, because I prefer this way of living. I often have difficulty sleeping at night and so I get up and do many things. I watch TV, go to get ice from the fridge and I make some noise. This creates a problem for others because everyone wants to sleep in order to be able to get up in the morning. So, it's easier for me to live alone. However, my wife, my children and my four grandchildren all find that dialysis is doing me much good.

Another thing that has happened since I started on dialysis is that I've regained my appetite. Unfortunately, after the treatments started, I immediately had to see a dietitian who forbade me to eat certain foods that I like very much. Often I just can't resist and I eat some of the forbidden foods. I know that this isn't good for me, but it's hard to resist sometimes.

I find that dialysis is very good for me and I like it because now I feel really well... At the beginning I didn't feel anxious because I had gone to visit the dialysis centre before starting and the other patients there told me that it didn't hurt at all. Before starting on dialysis I often had nightmares and I had noises in my head, but now that my blood is well cleaned by the dialysis machine, all this has stopped and I am very happy about it. When the kidneys have stopped functioning dialysis cleans everything up and afterwards you really feel great.

90

Anneliese Rabe, a 74-year-old woman, began hemodialysis six years ago.

Each person is supposed to be born with healthy kidneys. They are as important to life as your heart or lungs, but sometimes they stop functioning due to kidney disease. That is what happened to me, although I never realized that I was developing kidney disease, because I had no aches or pains. I used to try to stay away from doctors as much as I could. Then, about 15 years ago, I had a stroke. I was referred to a neurologist who gave me a check-up and referred me to an internal medicine outpatient clinic. I was given another check-up there, and I was told that I had problems with my kidneys. I was also diagnosed with various other problems, such as diabetes and high cholesterol. I was then sent to a kidney specialist, who confirmed my kidney problem and followed me up for the next few years. He saw my kidney function go down over the years, and kept track of the percentage of my kidneys that was functioning. He explained how some of the symptoms I was experiencing, like having a bad taste in my mouth, were due to the reduction of my kidney function. Eventually, he told me that it was time I had a fistula put in, and that was when I started dialysis.

Really, I didn't have many sources of support during this time. I have to say that I also had breast cancer a few years ago, and that I had to have a radical mastectomy of my right breast. That is one thing which really prepared me to deal with dialysis, and which helped me to cope with it. Also, I am very strong when it comes to willpower. That is really what helped me to deal with what happened.

I think that people should take dialysis from day to day. When I come to the dialysis unit and I see people who complain all the time, I feel sorry for them. I don't think that this is how it has to be. In situations like this, I think people have to help themselves and cope with their problems. I think that people should first get on the machine, and then see how they cope with it. It's true that dialysis is not perfect, and I have had problems with it too. Sometimes, my fistula gets clogged, or there is trouble in needling it. Other times, my blood pressure drops very fast, and  this causes me to pass out. I also get tired and have problems with my legs. But that's how it is, one day you don't feel so good, and then the next day you feel better.

To me, what is important is listening to the doctors and following their recommendations, so I make sure to always do that. It's true that doctors are not God, but they have studied and they are supposed to do the best they can for their patients. So I think that it is important to follow their advice, and when there is a problem, they are the ones to talk to.

91

A 47-year-old man who wishes to remain anonymous began treatment 17 years ago. His treatments have included hemodialysis and two kidney transplants.

I found out that I had kidney failure in May 1979. At that time I felt that I had some weakness, some pain in the bones and pain in the back. As a physician I didn't want to know exactly what I had. I decided to take an x-ray of the back because I felt pain in the back. The report indicated that I had small contracted kidneys. I checked my blood urea and creatinine and they were very high, so I realized that I had kidney failure. At that time, I was in the Middle East and I decided to get another opinion. I was investigated in London and they said that I had to plan to have hemodialysis. At that time peritoneal dialysis was not a real option. They prepared an access for hemodialysis on the right arm but the access was a failure. I went back to the Middle East and at that time they had recently established a transplant center in Kuwait. All my family members were ready to donate a kidney for me. Finally, one of my sisters was found to be suitable. Before I had the transplant, they made me a temporary shunt and I went on hemodialysis for about six weeks. The hemodialysis was terrible. It was really painful in the sense that you feel incapacitated. You feel dizzy, sick, weak and you feel like you want to vomit.

Finally, in October 1979, a transplant was performed and I stayed in the hospital for a month or so after which I was feeling fine and my biochemical parameters for kidney function were normal. I started to enjoy a normal life again. At that time I was at the end of my residency in Pediatrics and then I started my training in Genetics. Regarding my professional life, it wasn't a major setback because it occurred only towards the end of my residency. I was married with a child at the time. My wife's reaction was one of sympathy and love. Maybe the disease was present for six or seven years before I knew about it. Being a doctor you know almost everything and because of that you don't want to ask questions.

Sometimes you just don't want to know. For example, when you go for the transplant you know that it will result in either success or failure. Sometimes the kidney is rejected. You need patience and courage, and a strong faith to deal with things.

My relationship with my whole family was really excellent. After the transplant the relationship with my sister became even more special. My kidney started to deteriorate to the point of renal failure once again in 1994 after almost 15 years. The doctor decided to put me back on dialysis. The choice was peritoneal dialysis which is done at home. I had the access in my abdomen. I started dialysis in June 1994. I was on the list for a transplant. I didn't stop working. Nobody knew that I was on dialysis. I came to the hospital just for check-ups. After my transplant, I had another three children. I had a son in CEGEP and a son and daughter in secondary school and another daughter in elementary school. They accepted it. They understood that I needed it and they were sympathizing with me. I was doing dialysis four times a day. It would take me half an hour or sometimes 45 minutes each time. It was tiresome but I decided that I was going to face it and continue my work and that I wasn't going to take any absences. I was continuing·my duties at the hospital and I continued my teaching.

In August 1995, after about 15 months of waiting for a kidney, I came to the hospital and they told me that they had found a suitable kidney. Before the operation, I had mixed feelings. I was happy, and I was scared. Sometimes I thought why should I even have the transplant? But I thought that the transplant would save me from doing dialysis four times a day and it would make my life easy. Even on dialysis, I would attend conferences and I used to travel. I got through it with the help of God and my wife who was very supportive. I experienced a lot of problems after the transplant. I went into acute rejection. It was a short distance between life and death. After about two months I became better and left the hospital. After a month I went back to work. Now I feel great. I have always viewed myself as normal because I have always felt that it is one's mental health which is important. This is something that just happened to me without it being my choice.

92

Gerda Farkas, a 82-year-old woman, began hemodialysis six years ago.

I have been on dialysis for six years. Everyone at the hospital is very nice. I have very good doctors. But there is one nurse who is very mean to me. For example, every morning I prepare all the needles that the nurses need on the table to help them out and they all appreciate it. If I can do something to help then I do it. But this one nurse does not like it when I prepare the table and she tells me not to do it. Every day she finds something else to complain about.

When they told me that I had to go on dialysis I was afraid. When they first put the needles in my arm I was screaming because it hurt so much. Now everything is okay. I have to do this and so I do it. Dialysis has saved my life and I am very happy. My family was also happy when I went on dialysis. Before dialysis I was very sick and now I feel much better.

I live with my granddaughter. She helps me in every way. She makes sure that everything is okay. She always tells me to go and rest because she knows that I am very tired after dialysis. At the hospital I only eat dessert and when I go home I have my lunch. My granddaughter will cook meals without salt. I have one great-grandson who is one year old. I watch after him sometimes and it's tiring because he is so full of pep! He gives me a lot of happiness and pleasure.

93

Marcel Brunet, a 70-year-old man began, hemodialysis six years ago.

I have been on dialysis about six years. I was in the hospital for many things. I have heart problems and a ball on a main artery. They can't operate because my heart and my lungs are too weak. Six years ago I was vomiting green stuff. I didn't know what I had. I didn't want to come to the hospital for that but my wife and my son-in-law said that I had to go so I went. They didn't find out what I had right away. About three days later they sent me down here to try out dialysis and it worked. They told me that my kidneys were finished. When I found out that I had to go for dialysis I didn't think about it. I was sick so I had to do something. When

I started dialysis I was in the hospital for a couple of nights and I had doctors on both sides watching me all night. In the morning I had tubes put into my throat. My family thought that it was better that I come for dialysis because if I didn't come I would have died.

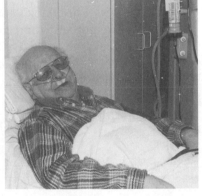

When I worked I used to sand the floors and the alcohol we used to put on the floors was very strong and that didn't help me out. I started smoking when I was very young. We used to steal cigarettes from my father at seven years old and go and smoke them in the woods. I quit smoking 12 or 13 years ago because of heart trouble and I nearly died. I wanted to go back to work but the doctor didn't want me to because my heart was too weak. The only thing that I don't like is that my heart is too weak.

My wife is at home. She's sick too. She has heart trouble but she does more work in the house than I do. My younger brother helps me out. I didn't want to put Christmas lights all around the house anymore but my younger brother put them up. There are about 500 lights. Everybody comes to see my house. People bring their little children to look at it.

I can't work anymore. Once in a while I choke because I drink too much water. I have to go to bed often. It's not the same life. But I help my wife with the dishes and I put them in the washer. In the spring and summer I try to work on my garden. I have a big garden. My wife helps me with that. It takes us a long time now. What we used to do in one day now takes us three days. Next year I don't think that I will be able to do it because I'm losing my breath all the time. I have to stop every five minutes and rest for half an hour and go back for another five minutes. I'm going to try to get somebody to do it for me because I like to garden. I like to see it grow. It's nice.

I would like to tell new patients that dialysis doesn't hurt and it could save their lives. Without dialysis I could die in two weeks. Make dialysis a part of your life and live a good life after. That's what I'm trying to do now. I'm taking care of myself and so is my wife and my daughter so I've got help. In the old days they didn't have dialysis and people died. Today we could live for 20 years or more. Don't quit. There was a man who walked with two canes and he used to whistle for us. I don't know why he signed the papers but he quit dialysis and died. I don't know why because he was happy here with us. I'm a little bit sick now but I'm still alive and with my family.

94

An 81-year-old man who wishes to remain anonymous began hemodialysis four months ago.

About four months ago, a check-up at the doctor's office showed that my kidneys had deteriorated to the point where I had to begin hemodialysis. This was a surprise, because I had not realized that my kidneys were failing. I had been getting a little dizzy sometimes, but I didn't know that my kidneys had actually stopped working. The day I was diagnosed was when I found out that I had to begin hemodialysis.

The hospital where I now receive my dialysis treatments is the same hospital I have been coming to since I was a youngster. That was back in 1927, but I haven't gone to another hospital since. Now I'm 81 years old, but I'm young! To me, 81 is just like 18 in reverse, if you play around with the numbers. With time, this hospital has become just like my second home, and I have made some good contacts here.

I have been retired since 1978, and two years ago I became a widower. I have three sons, and two of them live in different cities. One lives in South Carolina, and the other lives in Nova Scotia. They work, and they are kept busy. Since I started dialysis, I can no longer travel like I used to, so I am not able to go visit my sons. They both live in suburbs where there are no facilities for dialysis. So I'm connected to this hospital by the dialysis cord, and unfortunately the cord is not long enough to stretch all the way to my sons' homes!

Otherwise dialysis hasn't changed my life. It just added something to my life, by putting me on a program where I need to keep a schedule. I still do all my activities, but now they're scheduled around the three times a week when I have to be in the hospital. Yesterday, I just went carpet-bowling. That's like curling, except that it is played on a carpet. My team is the "Bobcats", and we're at the top of the league. When we played yesterday, we won the first two sets before we had to take a break. That is my main activity, but I also walk quite a bit. I don't walk as fast as

I used to, but I still manage to go on my walks. At the beginning, keeping to my new schedule was a change, but now it has become more or less routine.

I don't worry about being on dialysis. I know that it is doing me good, and that it cleans out my blood. The only problem is that dialysis leaves me tired. Sometimes, I don't want to do anything at all.

If someone is just starting dialysis, my advice is not to worry about it. Being on dialysis is not nerve-wracking, and it's not sensational. You just have to come in and get connected to the machine. Then, the important thing is just to allow for the change of schedule that will be required in order to come three times a week.

95

Juanito Lopez, a 33-year-old man, began hemodialysis five years ago.

My kidney troubles started when I was working on a ship as a steward. I started to have stomachaches, headaches, and I was vomiting all the time. I ignored these symptoms because I thought that these aches were normal and temporary. Later on, my eyelids started to become puffy and my ankles and face became swollen and I started to develop a bad taste in my mouth. I also started to have cramps in my legs. I said to myself this cannot be normal but the ship at that time was making a stop in the now former Yugoslavia, and the situation was not safe for me to go see a doctor there. I decided that I should wait until the ship reached Canada which was our next stop. As soon as I arrived in Canada, I went to see the doctor who took several blood and urine samples. The doctor finally decided to put me on dialysis. The following week, the doctors did a biopsy on my kidneys and finally found out that my kidneys had totally collapsed. During my first two weeks on dialysis, I did not feel any difference because I was so sick. My headaches and vomiting persisted and I was feeling constantly weak, and the bad taste in my mouth was still there. Right now my health condition has improved though I still have some headaches from time to time but I think that's normal.

Before I started on dialysis, I did not know what it meant. I had heard the word dialysis before because our President in the Philippines, Ferdinand Marcos, was on dialysis. I thought that I needed to take only two or three treatments in my life, and then I'd be fine. I did not know that I had to be on it for the rest of my life. When the doctors told me that I'd have to start on dialysis, and that I would not be able to work anymore, I was very devastated and I started to cry. I remember my first day of dialysis was on Friday, September the 13th, 1991 and I was pretty scared. I started to wonder what was going to happen to me. I was alone and I did not know anybody here. All my friends were on the ship and the ship was long gone. I was only 28 years old and the youngest patient then on dialysis and I found it too hard to be sick at such an early age.

I was very fortunate because the head nurse at the dialysis clinic was from the Philippines and she and the other nurses provided me with everything. For instance, six months after I had been on dialysis, my insurance coverage finished and I had no money to pay for my expenses. The nurses at the hemodialysis offered me a place to stay and transportation to and from the hospital. The nurses even organized a fundraiser for me and I will never forget that. The hospital also assigned a social worker for my case and that also helped me get over my anxiety. I am still keeping in touch with my family, back in the Philippines, and they do all they can to try to keep my morale high, including sending me some Filipino food.

During a party in 1992, organized by a Filipino nurse who works in the hemodialysis clinic, I met a Filipino girl, and we later got married and now we have a two and a half year old baby boy. The doctors at the hospital used me as an example for those young dialysis patients who were worried about not being able to have children once they were on dialysis.

Although dialysis has limited my life, if it was not for it I'd be gone a long time ago. I consider dialysis as my second life and the dialysis machine as my partner. Once I am off dialysis I try to forget about it and that helps my morale. I was a good eater before but now I have lost my appetite and I don't sleep much at night. However the lack of sleep and appetite are also due to some of my personal problems. Dialysis did affect my sexual life but once the doctors put me on drug "X", my energy was boosted and I felt much better.

So as a word of advice to whomever wants to listen: don't ever think that you are too young or too strong to become sick. Don't hide from sickness if you do not feel too well. Seek medical advice. In my case I am always praying to God and that's important for me to keep my spirits up. I have my baby boy that I want to see grow up. Right now I spend a lot of time with him. I take him to the park when the weather is warm and we play together. You probably have people dear to you that you want to see, and only dialysis will enable you to live and to keep seeing those people.

96

Grace Patone, a 78-year-old woman, began hemodialysis 13 and a half years ago.

Except for having to come three times a week to the hospital, dialysis does not really make an impact on my life. I was a housewife when my kidneys failed so I did not have to cope with the loss of a job like some

people do. After starting on dialysis, I was still able to cook and take care of my house and husband. However, a year after I started dialysis, my husband died and that was tough for me. I lived alone for about four months until my daughter and her family moved in with me. I felt a little bit better because my daughter's family was there to keep me company and to help me in case I became sick.

Dialysis is hard to forget about because the day I am not on dialysis I think about the following day when I'd have to be on it. However I don't complain about it because I see it as a part of my life. Dialysis has become something like going to work. People go to work to make a living and I come to dialysis to stay alive. The days of dialysis go by quite fast because there is a group of Italian hemodialysis patients, who do their dialysis at the same time, and we talk and talk and talk until the dialysis is finished.

I think about the future but in a positive way. I want to see my great-grandchildren grow up and my grandchildren get married. Now is Christmas and come the spring, I will plant my garden and I'll do some repairs in my house. I do not think about dying and that's what has kept me going for 13 and a half years.

For those who are about to start dialysis, they need to be a little patient because it'll take them a few months before they can start feeling better. They should not worry too much about what is going to happen to them in the future and should take dialysis day by day. Eventually dialysis will not be as bad as they initially thought, and they will not regret their decision. They need courage to face up to dialysis and need to rely on themselves because they are the only one who can help themselves.

97

Stefan Krawczuk, a 78-year-old man, began treatment two years ago. His treatments have been hemodialysis and peritoneal dialysis.

I do not consider myself a hero. I think that the description of "hero" is something that people can only confer upon themselves, and right now I do not feel that I qualify for it. When I climbed the Alps with some of the best climbers in Germany, I considered myself a hero. Now, I am on dialysis due to kidney failure, which also involves difficulties. However, I don't think that I've done anything in this situation for which I would deserve to be called a hero.

I have been on dialysis for two years now, and this has included both hemodialysis and peritoneal dialysis. When I first found out that I had kidney problems, my reactions went through several stages. I think that these were very similar to the three stages described in books given to people who are about to begin dialysis. These stages are revolt, bargaining, and acceptance. I went through them in that order, but while I was going through them, I never believed that I would eventually reach the stage of acceptance. However, I did reach it, which shows that you cannot always predict what will happen.

During that time, if it were not for my wife, I don't think that I would have survived. She was there for me all the time, and I do not know how she did it. She used to stay with me until 11 o'clock at night, and at three in the morning she would come back. That made a real difference for me. Also, another source of great support was the nurses, who were always helpful. Even now, I consider them to be angels. They were always around to help, and they never hesitated to answer my questions.

Since I have begun dialysis, there have been important changes in certain areas of my life, and this has applied especially to the realm of my activities. I am a skier, and I used to practice both downhill and cross-country skiing. Now, I have had to stop because I have not wanted to take the risk of being on a hill alone in case there should be any problem.

Although I am still physically capable of skiing, I have not wanted to take that chance. As well, I used to practice martial arts, and most notably kung-fu, the oldest and hardest of the martial arts. I've had to stop that too, because kung-fu is a rough sport and I couldn't expect people to be more gentle with me because I was on dialysis. Finally, I used to swim in the lake at my country house, but have had to stop that to prevent any possible infections.

My advice to people who are just starting dialysis is mainly not to remain alone with all the information books they are given. I think that this should be avoided because people are upset at this time, and cannot concentrate on the books. That's why I think it's important for people to find others who can assist them at that time, if possible. I think it is important to ask questions about all the options available, and make sure to understand all the facts. I also think it could be helpful to speak to others who are going through the same experiences. This would not be to get any specific advice, but just to talk and exchange views. However, perhaps the most important part of the coping process is that which takes place within oneself. For me, the crucial step was to look deep in my thoughts and face what was happening. I'm not much of a philosopher, but I believe that each man has his own horizon in life. When I found out that I had kidney failure, I felt that my horizon shifted. I now had to lead a different type of life, and dealing with that was up to me. Ultimately, this was something that nobody else could help me to do. But I'm a fighter, and this has applied to all situations in my life.

I'm quite a religious person, and I believe that health is the greatest gift God can give a person. So it is a person's duty to protect it and take care of it. I think that this is the aspect which is truly difficult and requires real courage. Due to my religious beliefs, I believe that if someone is placed in a difficult situation, such as that of having lost a kidney, it is because he or she has been given a burden to carry. My reaction to that was to pray to God to give me the strength to carry that burden. However, no matter what the source of a person's strength, it is something which is important to have in this situation. That is because one must fight to overcome this challenge all the time, every night and every day. If a person does not train himself to fight hardships, I believe that he will not succeed. The most important thing that people must learn is how to help themselves.

98

Gloria Saragossi (1948-1996) received treatment for 22 years.
Her treatments consisted of a kidney transplant and hemodialysis.
Her story is told by her husband Albert Saragossi.

Gloria gave birth to Karyn December 5th, 1973. Gloria was at the time the mother of Michael, who was three years old. For a few months after she gave birth, Gloria was not feeling well, she was really tired. Eventually, she was taken under the care of Vic Hymovitch, a friend and a doctor, who took some tests, at which point he realized that there was a serious problem. At one point the doctor told Gloria that she had to come to terms with her own mortality, and she called me at the office, crying. I ran down to the hospital, and such was our first crisis. She lost both her kidneys, and was advised that she had a condition called post-partum renal failure.

They whipped out her kidneys and she was in the hospital for a while. A shunt was placed in her leg and we were introduced to hemodialysis. Again these were all strange new words, strange experiences and for basically kids, we were 25 and 26, just married with two babies, things were happening very fast. For some reason Gloria was determined to overcome it, by trying to understand her illness, what caused her illness, where she can get help with it, what she could do, what she could not do. She was tremendously strong and overcame a lot of medical problems.

Gloria was called in for a transplant. The transplant only worked for about six hours and then it rejected. The cause of the loss of her original kidneys must have attacked the transplanted kidney and caused massive rejection. Gloria came to terms with dialysis and three days a week she went to the hospital. At the beginning the dialysis was a process that took six hours. It's a terrible thing to go through, it's like going through a washing machine. If you set your mind to it, to knowing that this is the only way you are going to survive, I don't think it makes it any easier, but I certainly think it makes it worthwhile to tolerate. Gloria made it worthwhile to tolerate, notwithstanding the difficulties initial dialysis caused.

As the years progressed, technology improved but she still lived with going to the hospital three times a week. We adjusted to dialysis at the hospital, the unit became basically her family. The patients, the nurses, and the other staff became part of Gloria's life, and became part of our family's life. To the point that I was her husband, her partner, her friend, and bed mate and I did not see her as an ill person. A lot of my friends and clients would say at different times, "You must be very burdened to have a sick wife." I would say, "Are you crazy, she's the source of my energy and a lot of the inspiration for whatever I do." That was very true, it wasn't a party byline, it was exactly how it was.

Gloria was a great inspiration not only to us, but to many of the patients, and she certainly was a stick of dynamite in the dialysis unit. The doctors respected her, feared her, but respected her and she raised a lot of hell. She did so for an interest in herself, and an interest in the other patients and nurses on the unit, for better care and a better quality of life for all concerned with the dialysis unit. She tried to get as many people involved as possible in fundraising, in building up the unit, and building up awareness about kidney disease. Gloria was one of the founding members of the hospital's Kidney Fund, and a real whizkid at fundraising and driving everybody else to do fundraising. She was also instrumental in setting up the position of Renal Patient Support Service Coordinator. A peer support program was started three years ago and Gloria was really keen on it, she took training courses and was referred to several patients. She would contact people who were starting dialysis and were really anxious about it. This one lady named Suzanne called Gloria "her angel".

Gloria found out quite by accident in 1990 that she was afflicted with hepatitis C, which came from contaminated blood from one of the transfusions. Getting contaminated blood was a big fear that she had had for many years, but this is a natural risk of the many transfusions needed in dialysis. When she confirmed that there was no risk to others in her family of spreading the disease or being contagious, she decided to keep it to herself. This was an unbelievable show of courage or dedication, really a sacrifice. I was certainly upset when I found out about it. I found out about it on December 21st, 1995, when I came back from the Orient. I knew there was something going on because her condition was deteriorating. We talked about it that night. I asked her why she hadn't told me about it, and she then asked me what I would have done if I had known. I said, "Well I would have come back from the Orient." "But that's exactly what I didn't want you to do," she replied, "I want you to continue with your life and go on with whatever you are doing, you must continue." That was basically Gloria's credo, you have to continue with life, you have to live life to the fullest.

On the night of February 21st she was going into the operating room, with a carrousel of transfusions and needles sticking all over the place. Karyn asked her if she was scared, and Gloria said, "No". She was a hell of a lady, a great friend. Although physically Gloria is not with us anymore, she will always be with us, there's a very strong sense of her presence.

99

Henri Perron, a 28-year-old man, donated a kidney to his father Michel Perron.

It started in the summer of 1993, my father called a general meeting of the whole family in our house up north. That was the first time he had told the family that he had kidney problems. He was planning to go on dialysis. At that point I said to him, "Hey, you want a kidney, I've got two of them and I only need one, and you know, you could have one." So right away he said, "Yeah right, I'm not going to go and mortgage your life for my old carcass." I was surprised when he said that.

I only went to see my father on dialysis once, and I wouldn't wish it upon my worst enemy. It really hurt me to see him there. I think dialysis is good because it helps people prolong their lives, but I don't think that it really helps anybody, it's just a waiting room until you can get another kidney, because the ultimate solution is a kidney.

Going back as to why I wanted to give my kidney to him... I was not the model child, I had a very rough past. I was heavily involved in cocaine and drugs. I was very, very lucky to get out of it, I should be dead today, and I have a brother who died from it. Once you get into that kind of world, it's very, very hard to get out. Most of the time people's parents are not supportive in these types of situations, but my parents were very understanding and my father, he never gave up hope. I was able to turn around. Looking back on it, I am very ashamed of it. I had no morals at that point in my life. Afterwards, I was always thinking to myself, "How could I repay my father, how could I repay my family?" I always felt the guilt, it was always there. Every time I was at a family gathering, I could never look at my mother or my father eye to eye, I always felt that I betrayed them. When the opportunity came up to give a kidney, in my mind, I thought, "Wow, this is the greatest opportunity to break even." I didn't feel this right away, but the day of the operation, when I saw the bag of urine hanging from my father's bed, I told him, "We're even now." Now I don't feel any more guilt, he saved my life and I saved his. Now we could have a fresh start.

After I had decided to donate the kidney to my father, my relationship with my family changed overnight. My father and I became very close. I think it added a bit of friction between me and my brother Claude, because Claude was pretty much the only son that was very close with my father, and had spent a lot of time developing that relationship. I came out of left field to offer my father a kidney. This was especially hard because I was the wayward son, and I was the last guy who he had expected to have a close relationship with my father.

I wasn't afraid of the surgery, but what I was most afraid of was what would happen to my father if the kidney was rejected. That would have been my biggest rejection. If I tried to save him, but I couldn't. I think that would have been the worst for me. I would have felt like a failure. But, I always thought in the back of my mind that everything would work out.

My father had an operation before the transplant, which delayed the procedure. That was really tough for me, mentally. I was waiting and waiting, and thinking that I want to do this before I change my mind. You really have to prepare yourself mentally for an operation like this. I went into the hospital 100-percent healthy, and when I got out of there I wasn't even able to walk. I think the person who was the most worried, out of everyone, was my mother. She has her husband and her son on the table, so she had more to lose than anybody. She didn't have any control, and she couldn't make any decisions. I had decided that I would give a kidney and my father had decided to accept it, but she couldn't do anything except stand by and watch.

Today I do two hours a day of volunteer work, and I don't do it for me, I do it to help people, but in reality, I think that I do it for myself, because at the end of the day I feel great. I am involved with the Kidney Foundation, and the Maison des greffes du Québec, which is a house for people that are awaiting organ transplants here in Montréal. We provide a lot of helpful services for them at a minimal charge, so that they can concentrate on healing themselves and keep their mind off their finances. I also volunteer at the Fondation Jean-Lapointe, which is for alcohol and drug abuse. Most people that get involved with volunteer work choose something that has affected them personally. I work everyday to demystify organ transplants. A lot of people are against organ transplants and against giving away organs once they die. People don't realize that once you die, you don't need your organs, and by giving them away, you may not be saving a life, but rendering the quality of life that much better for someone that needs it.

I like the fact that I was able to get closer to my father, especially in the context of the family business. I feel fortunate in this situation that both parties want to work together. So it is a lot of fun. If he was still sick, I don't think we would be doing what we are doing today. We are proud of what we have built up and what we have contributed to society.

100

Michel Perron began treatment four years ago when he was 60.
He has undergone hemodialysis and a kidney transplant.

When I started dialysis in November '92, I was very weak, I had lost a lot of weight. I always wondered why the doctors did not start me on dialysis sooner, instead of making me wait until I felt really ill. Maybe they make you wait until the end so that when you start dialysis you feel better, so that it is a sort of a delivery. When you start dialysis the needle is very painful, but after the treatment you feel much better, not quite right away but the next day. You remove some of the water and the waste

 of your body. I was feeling great, I was getting stronger, I was able to walk better. When I started dialysis, for me, there was an improvement in my life. I did not like the needle, or being on dialysis, but on the other hand, it was always for the better. I was always going to the hospital, looking forward to it, because it is doing you

good. Especially at that point in time my kidney had really let me down, I was urinating very little, so I suffered more from swelling, which dialysis helped with.

Not too long after I started dialysis the ski season came along, and I was able to ski on dialysis, but not as I had before. I was doing a few hours of skiing in the mornings. As I ski in Québec City, I had a problem because my days of dialysis were Monday, Wednesday, and Friday, and I was on the late shift. You don't choose the time you get your shift and this was the time available. When I went on dialysis at night, I would have a problem going to Québec City. I would have to wait until the next day, but then I would arrive at the ski center too late, because it is quite a ways to drive or fly. So I managed to find a place in Québec City where I could get my dialysis on Saturday afternoon. I was able to ski Saturday morning and have my dialysis at 12:30 in the afternoon, then ski on Sunday, and come back to Montréal. That was good for my morale, because I felt that I was sick, but despite this I could still do the things that I was doing before, like skiing with my friends.

When my children came to see me on dialysis, some of them were shocked and surprised. When you see the tubes with blood coming from your body it always creates an impression on people. When my youngest son Henri saw me there, I could see his face turning white, and he said, "It doesn't make sense, Dad, I understand that you can give a person on dialysis a kidney, and I would like to give you a kidney to get you out of dialysis."

So this is how the transplantation discussion took form. You see my youngest son, Henri, expressed the desire to give me a kidney. In the meantime I had read some books about transplant. I read the testimony of people receiving a kidney and of people giving a kidney, and there were a lot of benefits of course for the receiver, but also for the people donating a kidney. Whatever the reason is for a person to give a kidney, it's a real gesture of love. There is an old saying that you enjoy more when you give then when you receive. I was still reluctant to accept the kidney from my son, because I wasn't yet sure about the consequences for his health. I had an expression at the time when he talked to me, he would say, "Dad, I want to proceed and go ahead with this", and I would say, "Take your time, Henri, I want to analyze this, I don't want to mortgage your health for an old carcass like me." Henri used to laugh when I used to tell him that.

It turned out that both children were compatible to be donors, about equally. This was not far from Christmas time at the end of 1992. The family met together, and I had a problem, I had two donors, but I could get only one kidney. My doctor, a real wise man, said, "If you receive a gift from your children, and it's the same gift, you should make them decide who will make the donation, because it's you that will receive the gift." I thought this made a lot of sense, so I told my two children about that, and they said that they would let me know the answer at our meeting around Christmas time. At that time they decided that it would be Henri, who was the number-one volunteer. He was the youngest son, who had the least responsibility. My other son was married with children and had many responsibilities at work. So we proceeded to make preparations for the transplant.

We were hospitalized two days before the transplant in the same room. This was quite a unique experience. It was something that I enjoyed. It sort of brought together two humans. You become closer, we sat in the room together, one of us in perfect health, who's there to give me a part of himself, and me because I need this part, and it's a relation between father and son. It had a lot of emotion, beautiful emotion, it was like living in a dream. Two days later we went down to the operating room, Henri left about half an hour before me, and we shook hands before we went down, wishing each other the best of luck. I was hoping that nothing would happen to him. After the operation I was taken up to the room and I was only half awake. I looked up and said, "Hi Henri, how did you do?" "Fine. Dad, the kidney that I gave you is working." I said, "How do you know that?" He said, "You have a bag beside your bed, which urine is dripping into."

One thing that you have to keep in mind is that when somebody gives you a kidney, the donor suffers more than the receiver after the operation. I received the kidney in front, in my abdomen. In the donor, they have to cut through your back and cut one rib, to get the kidney out. It is a bigger operation for the donor. For me it was only a 12-inch cut, and you have less tissue in your abdomen than in your back. So after the operation Henri was unable to move. I was out of bed the next day, taking a few steps, walking to the washroom, but it took Henri a good three days before he could get out of his bed, because it was painful. It stayed painful for him longer then it did for me.

I went home on Easter Day, I was very happy to go home. I recall the following day I was so proud that I could walk moderately, I started going to my office for about half an hour. Then of course it happened that while I was there some of my friends had called to find out which hospital I was in because they wanted to pay me a visit. The secretary would answer the phone and say, "Well, if you want to talk to him, he is right here in his office." They would say, "What, his office?" She would tell them, "It's okay, you don't have to go to the hospital to visit him, come to his office it won't disturb him!" It's fun in a way to let your friends know that you are out of the hospital and having a good recovery.

After a few weeks I was able to walk more, and slowly I was able to walk half-way to work. My energy and liking of work had come back. After two months I was almost back to a normal life. I was feeling good about life, and I really felt like doing something. People were surprised to see me so well, and I was glad to talk to them about the good of a transplant, because I wanted a few of my friends to put their names on the donor list and to think positively about the benefits of a transplant.

Six months after the operation, I was invited to assist in a presentation where two explorers were showing a movie of their trip that they had made skiing through the Arctic Ocean to the North Pole. When I saw the presentation I thought, "What a nice challenge, the beautiful colors of the Arctic, the ice, the storm and everything that goes with an expedition like that." They told me that they were organizing a short expedition for the following year. When I made the decision that night that I would go on this expedition, I forgot I was sick, I saw myself as an explorer. After talking to the explorers I realized that I had forgotten to tell them that I had a transplant. When I did mention this to them they were very skeptical. After a while they suggested that I discuss it with my own doctor. The doctors that I had spoken to in Canada were not available for the trip (especially after watching the film of it). It turned out that one of the explorers, a Russian man, was a medical doctor, and I had asked him to come to Montréal to meet with my doctors, in order to reassure us that he understood the disease I had, and he would be of service if I had a rejection. That convinced my wife that I could go.

The expedition to the Pole lasted a couple of weeks. We first flew to the former Soviet Union, and spent three days there briefing and getting to know the members of the group. We then proceeded north by airplane and helicopter. It took us about three days to reach our destination. We landed at the 89th parallel, which is one degree before you reach the North Pole. The trip was hard for me, but I made it, I followed the group. It was pleasant. It was a big challenge for me. I had to carry a 30-pound pack on my shoulders and 20 pounds on my sled.

What the trip did for me was that it helped me to train myself. If I had not had an objective I would have never trained so hard. I trained for six months prior to the trip almost everyday. I was walking, climbing stairs, doing some gym work, and cross-country skiing. I had proven to myself that I was back in good shape. It impressed my friends on dialysis. When I came back I went in to see my friends on dialysis, and I could see the look of envy in their eyes, and this is what I wanted to provoke. I wanted to make them realize that you could be ill, like me who was sitting beside them before, and a year later I was standing at the tip of the North Pole with a flag for the Kidney Foundation. This was a great moment. When I showed them pictures, some of them were skeptical, and I did not do it to hurt them, I just wanted to excite them, and prove to them that with some luck and willpower you can come out of dialysis and conquer some challenges. However, this was not just a one-time occurrence. The following year I made a second expedition for eight days in the South Pole.

For me this was the beginning of a second life. Before I had gone to the Pole I had started a business, and I had an opportunity to go bigger, but I said I would only decide when I got back. If my health was good enough to take me to the Pole, I knew I could take on bigger challenges. Since that time I have built up a business and it now has 1,700 employees. I have accomplished more in my second life than in my first. I sold my business when I was ill, but in 1994 I had started a new company and a business that is bigger now than the one it took me my whole life to build. This is something that I am proud of. I can only thank God that I have this opportunity, first to have generous children, and then of course to have the medicine that has made this possible.

In a way it is thanks to the Kidney Foundation, because today the research exists to make transplants possible. It only goes back 30 years, that people can be transplanted, and without that research I could not have survived. Dialysis goes back only 30 or 40 years, and before this the treatment was really primitive. Now dialysis can be done in a four-hour session, it works better, you feel better, and the science is more evolved. So I think the Kidney Foundation did a lot for people with this disease and I wanted to do something for the Kidney Foundation and for other people with this disease. This is my way of thanking them for what

I have achieved. I have become involved with the Kidney Foundation of Canada. I raised money each year with these expeditions to the Arctic, and I participate as much as I can. I realize that health is borrowed, it is not something that is given to us, it is lent to us. I think that life, disease especially, stops you, gives you time to become a little bit wiser, a little bit better. So you have time to think about a lot of things, your life, your family, your future. If you've never been sick before, when you lose your health, and if you get it back as I did, you appreciate it much more. This is why you become better after an operation or illness. You cannot ask a person in good health to appreciate what it is like to be ill, but after being ill, if you have the chance to come back, you are a better man than you were before.

About The Heroes Project Team

Heroes began life as two separate ideas which gradually merged into one.

Tom Hutchinson, nephrologist in the dialysis unit at the Royal Victoria Hospital and Professor of Medicine at McGill University in Montréal, became interested in narrative therapy and felt that publishing the stories of patients, as told first-hand, would be a powerful way for them to celebrate their life and achievements.

Sandra McCallum, Coordinator of Renal Patient Support Services for the Royal Victoria Hospital Kidney Fund, was looking for a good education tool for kidney patients, preferably in book form, which would provide a true picture of living with kidney failure.

Many discussions later, the idea of producing a book called "Heroes" was born. Elana Shapiro, a volunteer at the Dialysis Unit, became Project Assistant, and Helen Bocti, Renal Nutritionist with the Dialysis Unit added her considerable organizational abilities to the team. Helen Lewandowski and Dorothy Opatowski joined the group in a multitude of capacities including administration and interviewing. Other team members include Jody Zack and Adnan Elcorchi who interviewed patients, Verna Dottin who provided accounting skills and Diane Gaudreau who typed the manuscripts.

The Heroes Project Team
Back row from left to right: Dorothy Opatowski, Elana Shapiro, Verna Dottin, Diane Gaudreau
Front row from left to right: Sandra McCallum, Tom Hutchinson, Helen Bocti

Glossary

Antirejection drugs: Medications that help to prevent rejection of a donated organ by suppressing the patient's immune system

CAPD: Abbreviation for Chronic Ambulatory Peritoneal Dialysis. It is a form of dialysis performed by the patient in his/her home and in which the blood is cleaned by putting fluid into the patient's abdomen and allowing the inside lining of the abdomen (called the peritoneal membrane) to act as a cleaning filter.

Catheter: A Silastic® (trademark used for a soft, pliable plastic) tubing placed in a vein or the patient's abdomen in order to do dialysis.

Compatibility for transplant: A condition necessary to ensure that a kidney transplant is a success. The patient receiving the donated kidney must not experience too much of an immune system reaction, or rejection. There are less chances of such a reaction occurring when the donor of a kidney and the patient receiving the kidney are compatible—that is when they have similar immunologic features (or markers) on the surface of their cells.

Cyst: A bubble filled with fluid in the kidney or other organ.

Dialysis: A process of washing or cleaning of substances that accumulate in the blood when the kidneys are not working.

Fistula: An artificial connection between an artery and a vein created in order to enlarge the veins to allow for hemodialysis.

Hemodialysis: Dialysis performed by a machine that cleans the blood using a filter designed for the purpose.

Kidney transplant: A surgical intervention (or operation) in which a kidney from another person (either someone who has died with healthy kidneys or a living donor who gives one of their own kidneys to a relative) is placed in the lower abdomen of the patient to replace the kidney function that the patient has lost.

Kidney transplant donor: A person who gives a kidney to another person.

Nephrologist: A physician specialized in internal medicine who sub-specializes in kidney disease.

Peritoneal dialysis: A kind of dialysis in which the blood is cleaned by putting fluid into the patient's abdomen and allowing the inside lining of the abdomen (called the peritoneal membrane) to act as a cleaning filter.

Permcath: A kind of catheter placed in a large vein and left there "permanently" in order to do hemodialysis.

Polycystic kidneys: An hereditary kidney disease in which the kidneys are damaged by many bubbles filled with fluid (called cysts).

Rejection: A process by which the immune system of a patient attacks a transplanted kidney because it recognizes it as foreign.

Self-care: A type of dialysis in which the patient carries out the majority of the technical procedures.

Ultrasound: A method of viewing organs inside the body by using sound waves.

If you enjoyed *Heroes-100 Stories of Living with Kidney Failure*, why not give a copy to a friend? Available directly from the ***Heroes Project Team***.

A convenient order form is supplied below:

☐ Yes. I would like to order:

_____ ($12.95)
   (copies)

Please add $2.05 per book for shipping and handling.

Enclosed is $_____.

Make cheque or money order payable to: ***Heroes Book***

Verna Dottin
Royal Victoria Hospital – R2.38
687 Pine Avenue West
Montréal, Québec H3A 1A1
Canada

Name: _____

Address: _____

_____

Province: _____ Postal Code: _____

Country: _____

Telephone Number: ( )_____

Or: visit our website at www.clinepi.mcgill.ca/heroes